When TV Came to Town

By

Steve Harper

Cover art by our son, John Harper

This book is dedicated to

my parents, Joe and Martha Harper

and

the fine folks who lived in Haskell, Texas

in the 1950's and 1960's,

who provided the friendship and the experiences

that made these stories possible.

Introduction

Stories are the threads that tie our hearts together. When I hear a story, I almost always think of something similar that happened to me. When I tell a story, people often say, "That reminds me...." And they launch into a story of their own. Stories are the way we know we're part of the larger human family. We're not as different as we think. We're closer than we imagine. Stories are the shortest distance between two hearts.

I'm part of the Baby Boomer generation—a huge group of people reaching retirement age, with mid-life behind us rather than ahead of us. Stories are one of our favorite ways of communicating. We remember stories after we forget facts. We tell stories to stay alive. When we live in our stories, we are ageless.

My generation will be the last one to remember a time before television—a time when you played outside until it was dark—a time when you pulled up chairs next to a radio to get the latest news or follow the exploits of the Lone Ranger. And then the day came--when TV came to town. We looked forward to the day, but we didn't realize that a huge line was being drawn across the universe—a line that would change everything.

So, it seems important to me to tell some stories that connect to that special time—stories from the late 1940's to the early 1960's—stories that will introduce some of you to a world you never knew, and remind others of you of a time that seems to have largely faded away. But more than anything else, I'm going to tell you stories that I hope and expect will cause you to say, "That reminds me...."

Steve Harper

1

Where It's At

Haskell, Texas is my hometown. It has at least one thing going for it that Lake Wobegon does not—you can find it on a real map. Just look 200 miles west of Dallas and 50 miles north of Abilene, and you'll be real close to Haskell. Alas, some maps no longer have Haskell on them, and that hurts those of us who lived or still live in Haskell, especially when the maps include Anson or Jacksboro. But you have to take life as it comes, and you cannot allow one omission to ruin your life. There are other ways to find Haskell.

On any map, locate the spot where US 380 (running east and west) crosses US 277 (running north and south)—that's Haskell, named or not. In fact it's the intersection that separated Bynum's Furniture Store and Sherman's Floor Covering Store.

Sherman's was the First National Bank when I was born, but it moved a block to the west when I was small. But since Sherman's and Bynum's are gone, you'd better stick with the highways. Landmarks are only good while they last.

You can also find Haskell by knowing what it's between. From east to west, it is between Throckmorton and Rule. And from north to south it's between Weinert and Stamford. I don't usually recommend this method for finding Haskell. Except for Stamford, the other towns are smaller than Haskell. You'll probably be able to find Stamford on a map. They have a Wal-Mart, and everybody needs to know how to find it.

You can also find Haskell by going there. You'll know you're in the right town when you enter from any direction and see a sign that says, "Home of 4200 Friendly Folks, and a Few Grouchy Ones." But no, that won't work. The Chamber of

Commerce has taken down those signs. Haskell doesn't have 4200 folks anymore, friendly or not.

But for me, there's only one answer to the question, "Where is Haskell, Texas?" I'll bet it's the same answer you'd give about your hometown. "Haskell is in my mind and in my heart. It's in my memories."

Come on along—I'll take you there!

2

When TV Came to Town

Television had been around for a while before it made it to Haskell, Texas. We knew about it before we saw it. One day, we heard that Park Woodson's Appliance Store would have one hooked up in the front window pretty soon. Come to think of it, we may have heard that the first television would be in the window at Barney Frazier's Appliance Store. I'm sure both men were trying to "get there first." Either way, this was big news in Haskell.

We made our plans to go downtown after supper and see "TV" for ourselves. But we didn't figure that nearly everyone else in Haskell had the same idea. On "opening night" by the time we got there, every parking place was taken, and traffic was circling the Courthouse square, waiting for a space to open, so interested folks could get out and make their way to the window.

We were patient people in Haskell. It was okay to wait while others took their turn. But we were also courteous people. We knew that two or three minutes were enough, and then it was time to move out of the way so others could have our spot. It was that way nearly every night for a couple of weeks.

But like everything else, the new wore off. Pretty soon you could pull your car right up in front of either store (Park and Barney both had TV's by then), and you could usually watch as long as you liked. If you preferred Zenith, Park's was the place to go; RCA fans headed for Barney's. Undecided folks went back and forth. We were one of the "back-and-forth" families.

Obviously, the purpose of all this was to sell televisions. And we had every intention to buy one. As more and more people purchased their own sets, the crowds thinned out even more. The Couch's were the first family to have a television in our neighborhood on Avenue H. It was an RCA. I really don't remember a lot about the set itself, but I'll never forget the antenna that rose into the sky in their backyard. It was the tallest antenna I'd ever seen. If you bought a TV, you had to have one like it, because the nearest station was more than 90 miles away in Wichita Falls, and the best stations were 150 miles away in Fort Worth. It would be a while before the "local station" (KRBC) started 50 miles away in Abilene.

Like nearly everyone else, we made fewer and fewer trips downtown to watch TV in the windows. But I did find more and more reasons to go over to the Couch's and spend time with my best friends, Riley and Jerre Sue. It was only a matter of time before we bought our own television. It was a Zenith. We made Park Woodson a happy man.

3

Saturdays

You didn't need a calendar to know it was Saturday in Haskell in the fifties. Just count the pickup trucks parked around the Square. If there were more than twenty five, it was Saturday. Almost like magic they came. And with them came a collection of some of the best people on earth.

Most came to shop and restock supplies. Farming and ranching did not allow folks the luxury of coming to town every day, or when the notion struck. No, Saturday was the day to get what you needed for the week. Merchants gladly obliged by having their shelves, aisles, and racks filled to capacity. Cash registers rang out the joyous sound that business was good.

In addition to regular sales, merchants had their weekly "drawing." At 3:00 p.m. everyone congregated on the

Courthouse lawn to see who had won the giveaway prizes. Just in case you didn't make it to the lawn, or had to leave early, no problem—you didn't have to be present to win. Tickets included your phone number, so you could be contacted. And every Thursday, the Haskell Free Press would publish the list of winners in its weekly edition.

Besides the economics, people came to visit. Saturdays were "catch-up days." Gossip is too negative and too small a word for all the information exchanged in the stores, on the sidewalks, and on the Courthouse lawn. Everyone went home wiser. Families had plenty to talk about the rest of the week—until they returned next Saturday. Telephone lines buzzed with the latest news.

Saturday was "break time." Both theaters did the kind of business they wished they could do every day. And in the summertime, the city swimming pool was so packed with people, you could only hop up and down—which is all you really wanted to do, since the city emptied the pool each Friday and re-filled it with fresh, cold water just in time for Saturday's crowd.

Long about 5 o'clock the noise would die down and the pickups would begin disappearing. We would never have "shopped until the midnight hour." Decent folks didn't stay out late. Besides, there was no need to "shop 'til you drop." There'd be another Saturday next week.

4

Shopping

Saturday was not the only shopping day. Businesses were open every day except Sunday. But Haskell didn't have any malls. For any of you reading this for whom "going to the mall" has become a way of life, I'll pause and allow you to give thanks that you didn't grow up in Haskell in the fifties....

Okay, to continue. Haskell didn't have any malls within a hundred miles. The first one I ever saw was in Fort Worth, but I'd heard there was a smaller variety in Wichita Falls. When I was six or seven years old, West Gate Mall opened in Abilene, billed as "the largest shopping center between Dallas and El Paso." All the stores were under one roof.

On my first visit, I was impressed with the "under one roof" bit. But by today's standards it was nothing special. West

Gate Mall was more like one big building with various stores inside and "streets" between the stores. The roof just covered everything. But never having seen anything like it before, it was well worth the trip. On the way home, I still remember thinking, "Haskell has almost everything that West Gate has." Sure, the mall had more of it, and it was closer together. But you could find it in Haskell. If not, a local merchant would be happy to order it. The mall was nice, but not necessary.

In fact, we had our mall, of sorts. We called it "the Square." A row of buildings on each side of the Courthouse. Instead of starting at one end and walking to the other, far away from your car, you simply started where you parked and worked your way around the Square until you came back to your vehicle. I always considered that a better thing than the "under one roof" approach.

But for me, the most important thing was that, in Haskell, the clerks knew you by name. They knew what you liked and disliked. They would give you pennies to put into the gumball machine. I never got that kind of treatment at the mall.

5

Stick Horses

They are not on anyone's endangered-species' list, but they are virtually extinct. You might still find a stick horse in an antique store, or in one of those restaurants that hangs items from "yesterday" on their walls. I saw a stick horse one time in a burger joint that erroneously claimed to make hamburgers like they did in the fifties, but tried to sell them at 1990's prices. But other than a handful of sightings, stick horses have largely disappeared from the landscape. I asked a boy the other day if he knew what a stick horse was, and he looked at me as if I were deranged. He had no idea what I was talking about.

But in Haskell in the early fifties, stick horses were a necessity for any pre-school cowboy or Indian riding the range. Every dime store had them in ample supply, usually in a bundle, protruding out of a holding barrel. Young mavericks would easily wear out three or four before they started kindergarten. They were, in short, the main means of transportation in the young "old West."

If you've never seen a stick horse, you probably have a generally-accurate picture just by the name. Stick. Horse. But just in case....here's a brief description. The stick was basic to all models. Store-bought versions had measured and painted sticks. Home-made versions were limited to whatever size and color your mother's old mops and brooms happened to be. If the length was a genuine problem, your dad could always saw the stick to make it as long as it needed to be.

Sticks were standard, but neither the store-bought nor home-made varieties were absolutely necessary. In an emergency, when your regular mount was shot out from under you, you could pull a limb off of a tree and gallop away uncaptured by the enemy. But as soon as possible, you had to retrieve your real stick horse and keep riding it.

Stick horse heads were where the real differences surfaced. Store-bought versions were made of vinyl, with button eyes, yarn for mane, and plastic reins. More-expensive models might be made of cloth, with leather strips for reins. Home-made varieties might have heads made by your mom, or they might simply leave the broom or mop head on the end of the stick. The stripped-down version was just a stick—no head—with, or without reins. The tree-limb model came as you found it.

I don't want you to think that stick horses were perfect; they weren't. Their main flaw was that they didn't sound like horses. They sounded like sticks dragging on the ground. To experience this for yourself, take a mop or broom outside and drag it fifty feet in any direction. You'll get the idea. To overcome this defect, each rider used his or her mouth to make the sound of a galloping horse.

Some riders made "clicking" sounds with their tongue and the roof of their mouth. These sounds were syncopated to approximate the rhythm of the hooves, speeded up or slowed down to suit the occasion. I personally preferred a slightly-above-whisper "goppety, goppety" sound—again syncopated to speed and need.

The sound of the stick horse has left the land. Their tracks have long been washed away and covered over with grass. But at night, as you lay in your bed quiet and still, you can let them run again in your mind: goppety, goppety.

6

Trains

People who only know trains like Amtrak, or those that have clever names like "the Japanese bullet," don't know trains. Like stick horses, about the only time you see real trains these days is when some railroad club pulls an old locomotive out of mothballs and sponsors an expensive trip to somewhere and back. There are a few tourist towns where trains still operate and carry passengers on "dinner runs," but that's about it.

It wasn't that way in Haskell in the fifties. Trains came through several times a day. There was no charge to go down to the depot and enjoy them to your heart's content. You didn't need a schedule. The engineer was kind enough to blow the steam whistle several miles outside of town. That gave you plenty of time to get to the main crossing and see the train, if you wanted to.

Those old "iron horses" were something to see. In the daytime, their clouds of black smoke instantly located them in the distance. At night, their boilers glowed orange while their headlamps swept back-and-forth on the track ahead. By 1950, the passenger trains were no longer coming through Haskell. You had to go to Abilene for that, and then you could only travel east or west. The trains that came through Haskell were commercial ones, hauling long ribbons of boxcars and tankcars.

Nighttime was my favorite time to see the trains. I can remember many evenings when we would hear the whistle, jump out of our chairs at home, run out to the car, and head for the depot. For a while, we did it so often I even knew a few of the engineers and conductors by name. If they were not in a hurry, they'd let me climb aboard and pretend to be an engineer for a few minutes. But even if they were speeding through town, on their way to somewhere else, they were still good for big waves and some extra toots on the whistle.

We didn't have any automatic warning signals in those days. There were white wooden signs, nailed in the shape of an "x" at the crossing. On the signs were the words, "Stop, Look, Listen." People knew you'd better do just that, and some folks even said the three words were a pretty good philosophy of life.

My favorite memory is watching trains uncouple cars at night. The signalmen walked up and down the tracks swinging their lanterns, telling the engineer exactly how to maneuver the rest of the train. It was a railroad dance, an art form in its own right, with the back-and-forth motions. Eventually the cars would be detached and the train would depart into the darkness with whatever cars were left. I remember standing on the tracks until the tail light on the caboose was just a little red dot. It always seemed extra quiet on the ride back home.

One day, I'm not quite sure when, the trains stopped coming, and I stopped going down to the depot. Some of the tracks have been dug up, and you have to know where they used to be to know trains were ever there. But I swear, every time I hear a steam whistle blow, I am instantly transported back to that crossing in Haskell, where I stood to watch the trains go by.

7

Cotton Fields

Our house in Haskell was bounded on the south and west by cotton fields. To farmers, they were places to plant and harvest cotton. But to me and my friends, cotton fields were our version of Disney World—complete with Fantasy Land, Frontier Land, Adventure Land, and Tomorrow Land. Cotton fields could also become Epcot, Hollywood Studios, or Animal Kingdom in the twinkling of an eye.

One day, cotton fields would be a war-torn island in the South Pacific. The next day, they would be the unexplored terrain of a distant planet. Before many days passed, they would be transformed into The Little Big Horn, where Custer took his last stand, or into The Alamo where Davy Crockett fought to the bitter end. At other times, they were sacred places to go and simply sit quietly in the rich, damp, dark soil. You could laugh and cry in cotton fields; confess sins or dream dreams in them.

My favorite thing to do was "play Army" in them. The dirt clods provided an endless supply of hand grenades, which would break into smithereens when they hit the ground. A lot of the time, the dirt was moist enough to dig foxholes and lie in wait for the enemy. When the cotton was high, the rows made great places to crawl on your belly as machine gun bullets whizzed inches above your head. Cotton fields could handle two lone soldiers trying to make it home behind enemy lines, or they could accommodate an all-day, Saturday military marathon complete with opposing armies recruited from all over town.

Later, I discovered that cotton fields had other values as well. At night, they were science labs where astronomy class was always in session. And still later, cotton fields were safe places to pull your car over with your girlfriend and "go parking."

Back in the sixties, someone wrote a song entitled, "They Paved Paradise and Made It a Parking Lot." I don't know who wrote the song, but I'd bet the person spent a fair share of time in cotton fields. There's just something good about dirt.

8

Go Karts and Motor Scooters

If the words "Simplex" and "Cushman" mean anything to you, chances are you grew up in the era of go karts and motor scooters. These wonderful machines gave dads more toys and moms more headaches than anything else around Haskell in the fifties. They gave a lot of children hours of fun and adventure.

Go karts are still around, but they're limited to commercial tracks, where people go to race them. In wild-animal language, that's like being put into a zoo. In Haskell, go karts roamed the streets untouched by law and order. But not for long.

Unbridled go-karting began to die the night the City Council passed an ordinance declaring go karts to be illegal for street driving unless they had tail lights and (get this) a windshield with wipers! Truth be told, we were probably creating a lot more danger than we thought we were. The City Council had to figure out some way to keep order in town and save our lives. It wasn't long before we sold my Simplex Go Kart in Abilene at a Go Kart Track to an Air Force airman. Jimmy Bynum put his home-made version into his garage.

But, no problem! Cushman to the rescue! The motor scooter was soon heard in the land. I had a steel-gray Highlander; Jimmy had a bright-red Eagle. These were our "wheels" until we turned sixteen. We went everywhere on our scooters, as far away as Rule (10 miles away). We knew the "thrill of the open road," including one day when we had to race back into town in a hailstorm.

Now that I am a parent and grand-parent, I see all the dangers I did not see at the time. If I had been on the City Council, I would probably have voted against go karts too, maybe even motor scooters. But sometimes God seems to overlook the ignorance of children, and He permitted our "wonder years" on go karts and motor scooters.

I haven't seen Jimmy Bynum in almost fifty years. But I'll bet there are nights when he gets quiet and stares into space. And for one, brief, shining moment, he and I are "rollin' down the highway" on the Farm-To-Market Road between Haskell and O'Brien, just north of town.

9

Steak Fingers

Some of you are confused. You're thinking to yourself, "I didn't know cows had fingers." Let me put you immediately at ease. Steak fingers are not cow digits. They are some of the best food on God's earth, and they were served up day-after-day in Haskell.

Steak fingers kept teenagers alive. You could get them on all four roads leading into and out of town. Elsie's Highlander (south), Woody's (north), Double A (west) and Dairy Queen (east). You were never more than two minutes from steak fingers. And if your car broke down, you could walk or even crawl to a place where hot steak fingers could heal your hunger and ease your pain.

Steak fingers are strips of tenderized cube steak, deep fried, and usually served six to eight on a plate with flour gravy, french fries, and Texas toast. My favorite version was served at the Double A, west of downtown Haskell. Even now, when Jeannie and I go back to Haskell, we hope the Double A is still open, so we can get our fix of steak fingers updated.

Steak fingers were more than food; they were the catalyst of teen-age social life. You visited over steak fingers. You shared young love with steak fingers. You cried on your steak fingers. You laughed with a mouthful of steak fingers. You split steak fingers and pledged to keep secrets to the grave. Football players plotted how to win the Friday-night game using steak fingers to diagram plays. Girls spelled out boyfriends' names with steak fingers—which probably explains why guys with short names had most of the fun.

So, you can see why I am really worried that steak fingers have all but disappeared. When is the last time you saw them? Or ate some? A while back, I almost caused a multi-car pile up on the Interstate. I looked down from an overpass and saw a little sign that read, "Steak Fingers." I failed to signal as I swerved down the exit ramp. But when I pulled into the drive-in, took my seat in a booth, and expectantly requested the large order, I was devastated a few minutes later when the waitress brought me some pre-fabricated substitute that would have made Elsie or Woody roll over in their graves.

Maybe—just maybe—it's not too late. If you know where there are real steak fingers (and you will know), write your Congressman and demand that the location be made into a National Park.

10

Radio Days

Lest I blow television out of proportion, a few words in praise of radio are in order at this point. If you are under fifty, you may have few memories of "life before television." You may have no direct experience of radio before stations became "Top 40" oriented, complete with FM stereo and "more music without interruption" than their competitors. When you add Sirius radio, and its rivals, to the picture, you hardly have an idea of what radio used to be. But there are still a few of us who remember radio differently…and…fondly.

The first radio I remember in our house was a Philco. It was old the first time I saw it. The case was wooden, rounded to a point at the top. The front was nearly all "face," with a lighted dial and cloth-covered speaker. The front also had two knobs on it—left one for volume, right one for tuning. We'd never heard of "clear-channel broadcasting" in Haskell. That kind of reception was rare. A steady hand and careful tuning could come close. But a cloudless sky was also necessary.

Radio had its music and news, but what I remember most were the "programs." My favorite music program was "The Grand Ol' Opry" broadcast live from Nashville, and boosted across Texas via KRLD in Fort Worth. My favorite dramas were "The Lone Ranger" and "Amos and Andy." I liked to listen to them in the dark, with only the light of the dial illuminating the room. They seemed more "real" that way. On Saturday mornings, as much as I liked to sleep in, I had mom wake me up in time to lie in bed listening to "Big John and Sparky." Ah, radio days.

The magic of radio was not in the set or the station, it was in the listener. Radio lived in the mind. It opened the imagination in a way television never can. Radio invited you to create the program—the characters, the location, the plot—everything but the sound. Only you knew what the Lone Ranger really looked like. Only you knew all the stuff that was in Fibber McGee's closet. Only you knew how Amos and Andy's living room was furnished. Only you knew how long and winding the deserted road was on Mystery Theater.

When TV came to town, something happened. I remember the first time I saw Amos and Andy on television. They were "imposters" playing the roles. They didn't look like Amos and Andy. But sadder still, the "real" Amos and Andy soon faded out of my mind as the screen versions overtook them. Millions of people now had one picture, but they had traded something in to get it.

Television tries hard. It spends millions upon millions of dollars (often for a single episode) to create on screen all the impressions and images that came for free into our minds through radio. Mega-bucks actors, sophisticated graphics, creative camera angles, complex plots—it's all there. But we could come up with all that in our imaginations.

A while back, I read Garrison Keillor's remark that the spark for "A Prairie Home Companion" began to dim when there was pressure for it to be televised. He refused. That was a "radio man" talking—a man who remembers, like I remember, radio days. And I might add, that after Keillor was off the air for a while, he had the good sense to make his comeback on the radio.

11

Pet Parade

Leash laws were lax in Haskell. There was no professional dog catcher. Our house was the last one on South Avenue H. That meant I had a lot of pets growing up, some who wandered into our yard and others who were dropped off nearby. At one time we had fourteen animals who called our place "home."

My first pet was a German police dog my parents had acquired before I was born. Not a very good animal to have around a small child, so I have almost no memories of him. My folks gave him away. A couple of years later, Blackie wandered into our yard and became my first "pet friend." He was a Heinz 57-variety dog, with black and white markings. He was a very gentle dog who would let you do just about anything to him, including tying a red bandanna around his neck when you were playing Cowboys and Indians. Someone poisoned Blackie.

Thunderstorms came quickly in West Texas, and sometimes they hit with a vengeance and torrents of rain. When that happens, ditches run high and wild with water. That's how our first cat came into the family. One night during a downpour, we thought we heard a feeble "meow" behind our house, near a rain-swollen ditch. Dad headed out into the storm with a flashlight. In a couple of minutes he returned to the house carrying a small cat, just barely beyond kitten stage. We dried the little thing, wrapping her in a towel and laying her on the oven door with it turned to the low setting.

That's how Missie came to live with us, and she stayed with us until she died of old age. Over the years, she blessed us with batch after batch of kittens, and she had a direct role in swelling our ranks to the fourteen I mentioned above. During that period those cats, kittens, and two dogs would line up around the back porch tuning up like a symphony orchestra calling us to feed them. In that mix of mutts, we especially came to love Inky, Missie 2, and Tom.

But it was Big Boy who exceeded them all—my "number one" favorite pet of all time. He showed up at our house not long after Blackie was killed. He still had a lot of "puppy" in him, and we took to each other right away. For twelve years I had no better friend on the earth than Big Boy. He stuck with me during my "kindergarten dropout" year. He waited patiently every single day while I came and went from elementary school, junior high, and high school—never a day when he didn't practically wag his tail off when I'd come home. Big Boy never did grow much. Like Blackie, he was another Heinz 57-variety dog, with black with brown markings.

He was an "outside dog," but whenever it stormed or on an ordinary night when the notion struck him, he would scratch on the door and we would let him in. During the day, when he was not patrolling the neighborhood, he took naps in the front yard in a hole he had dug himself under one of our shrubs. In the dozen years he lived with us, he wore a trail between our yard and the Couch's house, two doors to the north. Making these repeated trips also meant he was a good friend to the Ashes and the Chamberlains. Big Boy was kind of everybody's dog.

His major flaw was that he liked to chase cars. No, he *loved* to chase cars. Some days it seemed he lived to chase them. And he was good, too. But the years took their toll, and his abilities declined even when his desire didn't. One day, when I came home from school in my junior year, I saw his collar on top of a chest of drawers in our kitchen. Mom couldn't tell me. She didn't have to. Big Boy had chased one car too many.

I walked into the back yard. I don't think it ever was as quiet or felt so empty as it did that afternoon. Mom had called dad at his office, and he had come home to help her put his still body just over the fence in a spot that would make a nice final resting place for Big Boy. But they knew I wanted to bury him myself. I carried the shovel and dug the hole. I dug it deep so no critters could get him. Besides, by doing so, it took longer. I felt like digging forever, but I knew I had to stop at some point. I carefully put Big Boy into the hole, not all that different from his special napping place in the front yard. I buried him, and I buried a lot of myself along with him.

When I go to Haskell and drive by the house, I know exactly where he is—even though the city has created an alley behind our house. And though his trail between our house and the Couch's is long gone, I can see it, even if no one else can.

12

The Great Experiment

I've had them. You probably have too. It's one of those things you stand in line for as a child—just waiting your turn. I'm talking about Chicken Pox. I don't remember how old I was when I came down with them. I don't remember whether my case was mild or severe. I do remember my parents telling me over and over, "Don't scratch them!" and "Whatever you do, don't scratch the scab off the pox!"

They conveyed their warnings in the same tone that they told me, "Don't touch that wire!" or "Get out of the way!" They didn't tell me "why" I should keep my hands off the itchy bumps, but I could tell they meant business. I suspected that scratching a scab off would result in some kind of unspecified doom. So, I dutifully tried to find other things to do with my hands while I watched the bumps dry up.

Days passed. I don't remember feeling particularly sick. In fact now, having had children of my own, I think Chicken Pox is one of those diseases where the parents feel worse than the children do. I got to stay home from school, which I always considered a pretty good deal. I have one memory of sitting on the floor in my pajamas, playing with my toys—something an only-child considers a divine blessing.

One morning, near the end of my illness, I woke up. I was in a particularly strong analytical mood. Mom and dad's words echoed in my mind, "Don't scratch them!" But why? And what do you suppose would actually happen if you did? The tempter was hitting on all cylinders, and I began to think about finding one spot on my body that would never be seen in public. If there were a pox in that particular area, and if I were committed to only scratching a single bump, I became convinced that my act would not set off a chain reaction leading to the end of the world.

I found the area. And I found a bump there. Halfway between my knee and my ankle one tiny pox was drying up, which meant a first-class scab was raising its head above skin level. I gave it a good look, to be sure it was ripe for the pickin'. I pulled the covers up over my head, so if mom or dad came in, they would not know what I was doing. I carefully selected the finger I'd assign to scratch the bump—the index finger on my right hand. It had experience scratching other things. One more time the words "Don't scratch the scab!" raced across my consciousness. I paused to ponder the possible consequences of my action. Then….I scratched.

Nothing happened. The scab was so dry it fairly flicked off the bump. No pain. No regrets. No calamity. It didn't bleed. It didn't do anything. Only a small bowl-shaped hole remained on my left shin. That was it. Not to worry. I'd had plenty of cuts before. They always "healed up." I figured this one would too.

But it didn't. And it hasn't. That little bowl-shaped hole has stayed there for more than 55 years. Whenever I pinched it together, it snapped back into its bowl shape. It was such a perfect bowl shape that it seemed God had created it there on Day One when He said, "Let there be light." Over the years, it seems to have shrunk a little, but I think that's because I've grown some.

As I write these words, the little bowl-shaped hole is still in sight. I confess that I didn't pick the correct location. It is visible if I am wearing shorts—that is, "visible" if another person happens to fall down within inches of my left shin with his or her eyes fixated on the spot. No hair grows in the little hole. I know right where it is. I visited the location just a few moments ago. There were still no catastrophic consequences to my action. But my "Great Experiment" did yield the resulting data that parents do occasionally know things kids don't. I also learned that you don't have to have a good reason for everything you do...or don't do. Every time I look down and see that little hole in my leg, I think about things like that.

13

'53 Ford

Dad worked for the Federal Land Bank. Because he oversaw five counties, and because he drove on a lot of dirt roads, we had two cars. As I neared my sixteenth birthday, the "farm car" was designated as the vehicle that would be my first car. It was a light-brown, 1953 Ford. It could have been a brand new Cadillac or Continental as far as I was concerned. Once I got my driver's license, it would be "my car" every day after school.

At fifteen, Texas law allowed us to have a learner's permit. We could drive so long as there was a licensed driver in the front passenger's seat. Dad and I had a lot of fun (at least I did) during that year, and what I learned from him was as valuable as anything I learned in Driver's Ed. I'm almost certain that I passed the parallel parking part of the driver's test because of all the time dad spent with me on that one maneuver. He made two barriers by cutting off two broom sticks and putting them into paint cans filled with hardening cement. He paced out the distance of a regulation parking space, put the barriers at each end, and turned me loose on the project. The broom sticks were high enough for me to see them above the hood and trunk. The rest is history.

I've already told you that our house was the last one on South Avenue H. You could turn out of our driveway, go less than a hundred yards, and turn right onto a road that circled the cemetery. At some point, I convinced dad that it wouldn't be a major infraction of the law if I ventured forth on that protected route. Dad agreed, and that became my daily journey in the car all by myself.

One day, while putting the vehicle through its paces on the backside of the cemetery, I met "Bull" Barnett, our city policeman, coming toward me. He saw me; no doubt about it. I'm sure he knew I did not have a driver's license. We had met before during my go-kart and motor scooter phases. I figured I was done for. As we passed, he looked me square in the eyes. I fixed my gaze on the rear-view mirror, expecting to see his red lights come on. But they didn't. He let me keep going.

But I was shaken. As I completed the course and turned back into our driveway, I was so glad to have made it home without a ticket, that I didn't line up the car real well. I drove right into the small ditch in front of our house—in full view of dad, mom, and Troy and Nellie Ash, our next-door neighbors. My folks and the Ashes visited almost every day in the front yard; that day they were doing so during my solo vehicular adventure. Troy had a pickup. It didn't take much effort to get the car out of the ditch, but it did take a while to get the embarrassment off my face.

Not long after, with license in hand, the old '53 Ford became my main way of getting from "Point A" to "Point B." I used it for everything except dating. There was just too much farm dirt to expect any self-respecting young lady to ride in it. But outside of that, my first car did everything first cars are supposed to do.

When our son, John, turned sixteen, I facilitated his right of passage by giving him the keys to my "work car," a white Honda Civic. But the strangest thing, as he drove off in it alone for the first time, I'll swear it looked like a light-brown '53 Ford.

14

Closed for the Season

If you travel the backroads of America for several hundred miles, you'll almost certainly pass a drive-in theater. I'd be willing to bet it will be abandoned, left to the elements, varmints, and vandals. I'd also be willing to guess that the old sign out front might still have "Closed For The Season" on it. Like the last days of Pompeii, those old drive-ins seem to have been left by folks who intended to return, but never did.

We had a drive-in theater in Haskell. It was located just west of town on US 380, where the road curved slightly to the north on its way to Rule. The road has been widened and straightened, so it's difficult to remember for sure where the old theater once stood. But during my pre-school days (1947-53), my family made regular trips to it.

Weeknights, you could wait almost until showtime to get to the drive-in, but on weekends cars would have to line up to enter. If you timed it just right, you would be able to find a speaker not too close, or too far, from the concession stand. Down front, under the screen, there was a small playground, where kids could go and parents could visit.

Hit music blared over the P.A. system, and the aroma of popcorn and hotdogs became stronger as the start of the movie drew nearer. At dusk, the floodlights blinked on and off a couple of times, telling everyone to return to their cars. The theater manager hoped folks would stop at the concession stand on their way back, and most people did. It just didn't seem right to sit in your car empty-handed.

To make sure it was pitch dark when the feature attraction began, we first watched newsreels, previews, and intermittent advertisements reminding us of all the good stuff waiting at the concession stand. Fizzy drinks and pieces of popcorn floating in the air were often enough to lure folks back for one last treat before the show began.

Things formally got under way with the indispensible cartoon. Thanks to Walt Disney and Warner Brothers, most of our favorite comic book characters came alive on the silver screen. I always looked forward to Daffy Duck, but it really didn't matter. Bugs Bunny, Porky Pig, Elmer Fudd, Donald Duck, Mickey and Minnie Mouse, Goofy, and Pluto were all favorites. Sometimes they ran a second cartoon, and we didn't have to pay extra for it.

And then it happened….the main feature began. Larger-than-life movie stars appeared and held us spellbound for the next couple of hours. At the Haskell Drive In, I saw classics like "Shane," "Peter Pan," and "The High and the Mighty." Some of my radio heroes, like Roy Rogers and Dale Evans and the Lone Ranger and Tonto came to life and reminded us that the "good guys" always win. It was impossible to leave the drive-in and not feel better than when you came.

By the time I started elementary school, the drive-in had "closed for the season." It didn't happen overnight, but came slowly. It closed during the week, open only on Friday and Saturdays. Not long after that, it was gone for good. A new, indoor theater had opened in downtown Haskell, along with a second one a bit later. The drive-in became little more than a memory. For years, it stood proudly where the road bent slightly to the north on the way to Rule, reminding many of us of happy evenings spent with family and friends.

Little-by-little the wind and rain did their work. The playground rusted. The concession stand had its windows broken and its doors knocked off. Weeds grew where cars once parked. The big white screen was a dingy brown, and a lot of it was missing. When the highway department decided to widen the road between Haskell and Rule, the drive-in was torn down. But I swear, somewhere on that stretch of US 380—about two miles west of Haskell, you can still catch a whiff of chili dogs loaded with ketchup and mustard. And if you listen carefully, you can hear, "And a hearty high ho Silver…the Lone Ranger!"

15

Tornado!

The Texas Theater was a "summer festival" in Haskell in the fifties. For one low price, you could buy a book of tickets that admitted you to weekly Saturday features. It was a great way to spend a day at the movies. It usually included a multi-week serial of some sort, the indispensible cartoon, and a feature presentation. All told, you could wile away several hours with your friends each weekend.

One Saturday afternoon, I had settled into an aisle seat with my Coke and popcorn. I became so glued to the screen that I hardly noticed the girl who walked up to me and whispered in my right ear, "There's a tornado coming, and we're going to blow away!" To this day, I have no idea who she was, or why she chose me to communicate that message. But for a moment,

I was the only person in the Texas Theater who knew this life-threatening information.

Within moments of her personal whisper to me, the theater manager had made his way to the front of the auditorium, turned on the lights, and gave an adult-version of the message I'd just received from the stranger—who, apparently, had spoken to me and then immediately turned and exited the premises. Since I had already heard the gist of what the manager was telling the crowd in a more detailed and peaceful manner, I didn't figure there was any need to hang around for a repeat. Besides, there were 200 or more kids in the movie. A head start was important.

As I rounded the corner and headed down the main ramp into the lobby, I tripped on an untied shoestring of my tennis shoe. Crashing headlong into the carpet, I laid there for a split second regaining my senses. It was just long enough for the remaining 199 kids to catch up as they too headed for the main exit. Each time I tried to raise myself from the ramp, a tennis shoe or loafer would slam me back down to the floor. I am not lying—I was the last person out of the theater!

Needless to say, the lobby and sidewalk out front were a madhouse. Parents had arrived and were frantically trying to pick up their children. The wind was howling and it was raining sideways. My folks were nowhere in sight. Someone called out to me, "The Couch's are over there. Get a ride with them!" Since they only lived two houses down from us, I figured that was the best option I had in the moment. I jumped into their car, along with Riley and Jerre Sue, and upon arrival, we all went down into the Couch's cellar to ride out the storm.

Unknown to me, my mom and grandmother were trying to get to the theater, but had to take their turn in the long line of cars waiting to get to the front doors of it. By the time they made it, I was long gone. Someone hollered out to my mom, "I think he went with the Couch's." Off she sped to find out for sure. Coming down Avenue H at a higher rate of speed than normal, mom attempted to make a sharp right-hand turn into the Couch's driveway. She made it, but the centrifugal force propelled my grandmother, who was riding shotgun, out the passenger door. I wasn't there to see any of this, but my dad later told me that my grandmother shot out of the car and then went bouncing on her bottom across the Couch's gravel driveway (this last detail is important to remember).

It all worked out. The storm passed without blowing anything away—as originally predicted by the girl in the movie. We didn't see or hear any tornado. When the wind died down, we exited the cellar. I learned that mom found out I was safe and sound. But dad, mom, and "Mamoo" were nowhere to be found. As it turned out, when grandma scooped herself up from the Couch's driveway, she discovered that she had multiple pieces of gravel embedded in her rear end—sufficiently deep to require immediate medical attention at our local hospital's emergency room.

Dad told me that Dr. Cadenhead patiently picked out each piece of gravel with tweezers, applied the necessary ointment, and sent grandma back to our house to let nature take its course. We were able to laugh about it later that day. But after all these years, I still wonder who the girl was who chose me to be the lone recipient of her "death" message. And I still have a tendency to look behind me whenever I get out of my seat at the movies to head for the lobby.

16

Television Debut

Pack 36 was home for about fifty Cub Scouts in Haskell in the fifties. About a dozen of us were members of Den 7. Together, we were making our journey from Wolf, Bear, to Lion—with silver and gold Arrow Heads added to the mix. We met weekly in Ed Hester's basement. His wife, Juanita, was our Den Mother. Other mothers pitched in too. Dads joined in as necessary, especially each year at the Pinewood Derby.

It was in Den 7 that I learned how to walk down a curb without losing my balance, how to build and start a campfire, and how to use a compass. But the most important thing that happened to us was receiving an invitation to be the guest Den on KRBC's "Calvin Kiwi Show."

The "Calvin Kiwi Show" was the weekly, live broadcast on KRBC-TV, Channel 9 in Abilene, Texas. Calvin was a bird. Actually, he was a large hand puppet who sat on the desk of Cousin Pogo. Calvin was also a cartoon character who would appear in a couple of episodes during each show. Just across from Cousin Pogo and Calvin sat a "peanut gallery" of special guests. These guests were interviewed and usually invited onto the show to perform in some way. The whole show lasted 30 minutes. But that was long enough, because in those days of live, black-and-white television, the studio lights were bright and burned hot enough to fry eggs.

Den 7 had been chosen to be one of the special guest groups. We would forever be known as the only Den in Pack 36 to appear on "The Calvin Kiwi Show." It was a big deal. From the day we received the invitation, until the day of the show, we engaged ourselves in passionate preparation, focusing on the demonstration of various arts and crafts that Cub Scouts would typically produce. Some were of the simpler type—the kind Cubs at Wolf level would make; others were more complex, befitting those Cubs who were on the brink of becoming Lions.

My assignment was to make an abacus, and then demonstrate it on the TV show. Within a week, I had completed the craft. The rest of the time preceding our trip to Abilene was spent rehearsing our presentations. In Juanita Hester's basement there was an electrical fuse box. We pretended it was the camera. When Mrs. Hester would shout, "Action!" we would take our turns staring into the fuse box, holding up our item, and telling the viewers all about it.

I confess, I was pretty good. Partly because I often pretended to be a TV reporter or news anchor. And partly because I had written a really cool presentation and committed it to memory. "This is an abacus. It was invented by the ancient

Chinese for doing arithmetic...." As I described the instrument, I moved the colored wooden beads along the thin metal rods that ran from one end to the abacus to the other. "By sliding the beads in this fashion, the Chinese could perform sophisticated calculations."

On the appointed day, we made the trip to Abilene and gathered in the KRBC-TV studio to take our seats in the peanut gallery. Calvin was already perched on the desk, but he wasn't moving, because Cousin Pogo had not arrived to stick his arm in the back of the puppet. Most of the lights were not yet turned on, giving the studio an eerie feeling not seen during the regular program. Technicians moved hurriedly throughout the studio, revealing the intricately complex professionalism of the moment. Something that looked fun and ordinary on TV was beginning to appear complicated and foreboding.

When the lights came on, I was already sweating. The room was stuffy and the air was thin. My Cub Scout uniform felt like it weighed a ton. The heat from the studio lights only intensified the problem in my stomach which had already begun. But I was excited. I had watched nearly all the previous shows. Today, I was on it! And I was ready.

The format of the show didn't put us on immediately. The bright lights became even hotter. My stomach felt funny. So did my head. During a commercial break, the director led all of us from the gallery to the studio floor, lining us up in a row. I would be the sixth or seventh Cub Scout to make my demonstration. When the show came back on, Cousin Pogo introduced Den 7, said how happy he was to have us on the show that day, and told the viewers what we would be doing.

With that, the little red light on Camera Two came on. Everything we had practiced so hard for was under way. I was really sweating now.   My yellow-and-blue Cub Scout neckerchief was getting damp. So were my socks. Kamikaze butterflies at 12:00 o'clock! Heading on a suicide mission for my gastro-intestinal tract. Funny, I had never noticed that the TV studio rotated when guest groups made their presentations.

One by one, each Cub made his presentation.   The camera would slide sideways from Scout to Scout, stopping in front of each presenter, about ten feet away from his face. I lost touch with all my senses as the Scout next to me was finishing his presentation. When the camera slid to the left to face me, I stared blankly into the lens and said, "This is an….uh… this is….uh….an….ab….uh…. an…. ab….uh………… Then, only silence. The camera waited at my position for a few more seconds; then it slowly moved on to the Cub standing at my right. My television debut was history.

17

One Short of Eagle

I recovered from my Cub Scout television trauma and went on to earn my Webelos badge and moved into Boy Scouts. Edd Smart was our Scoutmaster. We could not have had a better person to lead us. He loved the outdoors and all the activities related to Scouting, and he was dedicated to every Scout in Troop 36. He also had one goal: to see that every boy earned his Eagle Scout. In the Chisholm Trail Council he had more Eagle Scouts in his Troop than any other Scoutmaster.

I continued to advance, eventually earning my Life ranking. I took that rank with me into Explorer Scouting. I only lacked two merit badges in order to become an Eagle Scout— Swimming and Life Saving. My hope of earning them was fading away. I could not swim. In fact, I didn't really like to swim. As I've already told you, the Haskell pool always seemed to me to be too cold, too crowded, or too dirty. Even a round of swimming lessons had not kicked my swimming desires and talents into gear. I was far below the skill needed to earn either my Swimming or Life Saving merit badge. I had quietly accepted the fact that I'd leave Scouting with my Life rank and nothing more.

Besides my lack of skill, I was embarrassed. I was the only Scout my age who could not swim. I found a way to excuse myself from any swimming-related activities, including the annual summer week at Camp Tonkawa. I could not face another year of having to wear a white bead, which told everyone I was a "non swimmer." I made up some story as to why I could not go to camp, and told Edd I was not going to make it.

One afternoon, he called. He asked me point blank, "Steve, is the reason you're not going to Camp Tonkawa because you cannot swim?" I couldn't lie to him, so I answered, "Yes, Edd, that's the reason." He didn't let me off the hook, but continued, "Would you go if I worked it out so that you didn't have to swim?" I thought for a moment and replied, "Well, I'd really like to go to camp with my friends. So, if you can do that, I'll go." Edd responded simply, "OK, you're in." I hung up the phone thinking, "What a wonderful person and Scoutmaster to understand my situation and find a way around it."

But that appreciation disappeared instantly as I stepped off the Scout bus at Camp Tonkawa and heard Edd Smart tell one of the life guards, "That's him. He only needs Swimming and Life Saving to get his Eagle. I want you to see that he earns those badges before the week is over." I nearly passed out on the spot. Betrayed! But there was nothing I could do about it. I was 75 miles away from home with no means of transportation to get back there. I might have tried walking, but my legs were almost too weak to hold me up. Angry, hurt, embarrassed—you name it—I went with the camp life guard, retrieved my white bead (again), and enrolled in the Swimming Merit Badge class.

Don't forget. I could not swim. Everyone else but me seemed to have forgotten it, and when I brought it up, people acted like they couldn't hear me. Within less than an hour after arriving at Camp Tonkawa, I was already in the water with a personal instructor Edd Smart had put on my case! Everybody knew Edd, and they knew he wouldn't say it if he didn't mean it. There was only one goal: teach Harper to swim good enough to earn his final two merit badges.

Most of the week was spent just getting me up to speed. I was an official Camp Tonkawa "cause." A growing number of Scouts began to pull for me. One after another, they encouraged me: "You can do it!" they exclaimed. And by roughly the middle of the week, I had done it. I had swum the 150 yards, performed the "silent swim" maneuver, and done the other things required for the Swimming Merit Badge. When I actually went for it, the pool was bordered by nearly every Scout at Camp Tonkawa. They cheered when I finished.

I felt good—so good that I returned from Camp and went right into practice for my Life Saving Merit Badge. Within a week or so, I had earned it. A couple of months later, I stood with four of my friends in the Court of Honor ceremony at The Methodist Church. We were Eagles. I looked at Edd Smart. He had tears in his eyes. I did too.

18

Livin' Off the Land

Eagle Scouts are supposed to be able to survive in the wild. Jimmy Bynum and I had never had to do that, so there was always "something missing" in our being Eagles. We decided to put ourselves to the test. We picked a weekend, asked Ed Hester for permission to go onto his pasture, and packed our provisions. We were determined to live off the land.

After school on Friday afternoon, Jimmy drove his Chevrolet to the spot near Ed's tank (farm pond) where Troop 36 had camped on numerous occasions. It was familiar territory. We arrived about 4:45 p.m., which gave us about three hours before sundown. Our first items of business were to set up our tent and gather wood for the fire. We were off to a good start.

The next project was to snag our game for dinner. Ed's pasture was known to be teeming with potential food, but we had confidence that something would come along that we could kill and eat. Lo and behold, a jackrabbit obliged us. We moved up on the unsuspecting creature with the acumen that went along with being Eagle Scouts and members of the Order of the Arrow. Jimmy fired the fatal shot from his '22, and we carried our supper back to the campsite near the pending fire. We wrapped our potatoes in foil, confident that "Rabbit and Spuds" would be a meal fit for wilderness survivors.

Trouble was, neither Jimmy nor I had earned our Rabbit-skinning merit badge. There wasn't one. We stood over the lifeless animal never having seen it done, never having read about how to do it, or even having given much thought about ever doing it. The rabbit had done its part; we were the holdup. Ranking right up there with lack of knowledge was the lack of suitable equipment. In our haste to begin livin' off the land, we had failed to bring any sharp objects. I had a Scout hatchet and knife in my pack, but neither came close to having the razor's edge required for the task of separating the supper parts of the rabbit from the non-supper parts.

Jimmy had his Scout pocket knife in the glove compartment of his car. With it, we had a chance. If only we had any idea where to make the first cut—a decision which seemed even to us to be extremely important. We rolled the bunny over, almost like two guys hoping to find a "cut here" emblem, with related dotted lines. None was to be found.

Jimmy remembered seeing a deer "gutted" years ago. He was confident it happened on the underside of the animal. It made sense to think that skinning a rabbit would best be done on the same side. The sun was going down. We positioned the rabbit on its back, and spread it out as much as we could.

Jimmy made the initial incision. Wrong! We knew it without ever having had any rabbit-skinning experience. It was wrong. The knife had hardly entered the rabbit or moved down its belly before a dark, foul-smelling substance began to ooze out of the slice. Wrong! Definitely wrong!

Jimmy and I didn't say much while we sat in Elsie's Highlander about an hour later waiting for our steak fingers and fries to come up. We never again talked about livin' off the land. But I think we both felt sorry for the rabbit.

19

Sonny's

I'll be the first to admit that buying gasoline doesn't seem like an experience you'd remember for years. But in Haskell, it was different. Sure, there were the usual service stations with attendants who asked the standard questions ("Fill 'er up?"), and then proceeded to robotically do what you told them to do, or what they thought you told them.

But, at Sonny's you entered a new world of gasoline purchasing. Located just north of the Square on Highway 277, his station was there as far back as I can remember. Sonny Wilfong was 300 years old the first time I saw him. For more than twenty years, he never aged a bit. He only had two pumps—one for Ethyl and one for Reg'lur. Diesel was around the corner at the side of the station.

Sonny didn't have those hoses that make a bell ring when you drive over them. No, he was a real service station operator. He just "knew" when you had driven into his station. That's an intuition that only comes with 300 years of experience. Almost before your wheels stopped rolling, Sonny came huffing and puffing (literally, no other attendant in Haskell did that) to....your....car. He said not a word, but went straight to his work. That meant cleaning the windshield, checking all the tires and airing up any that were low (including your 'exter'—spare), and wiping all the outside mirrors and headlight covers. Before you could even exit the vehicle, Sonny was by your window asking how many gallons you'd come in for.

He always asked about your family, and occasionally talked about his. All his words and actions came between the huffs and puffs—along with a weak little whistle that would come out of his mouth with no predictability. And if by chance a few extra gallons poured into your tank before he could get back to the pump...no problem. He wouldn't charge you for more than you asked for. He wouldn't miss it, and you could use it.

Sonny operated his station in the days before key chains and ice scrapers had names on them. But he was ahead of his time when it came to marketing. As far as I know, no one ever left his station without a "block" (package) of gum—most often Wrigley's Juicy Fruit...no charge. And even if you didn't chew, Sonny knew that you knew someone who did.

I do not know if there are gasoline stations in heaven. But if there are, I have no doubt where I'll find Sonny. He'll be huffing and puffing whenever someone pulls in for a fill up. And he'll be sure to check your "exter."

20

Milwaukee's Finest

Every small town has its version of James Wheeler. Folks who've grown up in such towns know that what I am about to write is composed with nothing but the highest regard and fondest memories. This story in no way demeans James. Instead, it is my "from the heart" remembrance of a man who won a special place in our lives. It's not too much to say that we loved James Wheeler.

James was mentally challenged. None of us ever knew why. When I first met him, he was probably in his forties, but he had the attitude and behavior of a six or seven year old. Most likely, you'd see James on his bicycle. If it was summertime, he'd probably be heading toward or coming from a baseball game. Baseball was James' life.

He told everyone that he played for the Milwaukee Braves. He wore a dirty blue cap with a red bill, complete with an "M" on it to prove his claim. He would tell you that he had pitched that very day—and won. In fact, James was the star pitcher for the Braves. If you asked him if he had struck out every batter he faced, he'd answer the same way every time, with a drawn out, two-syllable, "yay-yah."

Once in a while we'd play harmless tricks on James, like telling him that the Milwaukee manager was on the phone, needing him to return to the diamond and be the game-winning relief pitcher. But most of the time, we were friendly with this quiet, gentle man. The only time I ever saw James agitated was when we would ask him more questions about "today's game" than he wanted to answer. He would either go silent and refuse to say a word, or he would hop on his bike and ride off somewhere else. But it wouldn't be long before he'd be back, talking about baseball some more.

It would be nice to know when you're seeing someone for the last time. You'd try harder to remember. But I imagine the last time I saw James Wheeler, he was riding off on his bike, heading for Milwaukee, to win another one for the Braves.

21

Satch

If you have ever seen a big fire, I'll bet you still remember it. For me, it was the night the Church of Christ burned down in Haskell. We were at home, but through the windows we could see an unusually large orange glow. It seemed to light up the whole sky to the north of town. We went out on the front porch for a better look. We knew it was something big, so we jumped in the car and headed out to find out what it was. It didn't take five minutes to get to the church, but it was clearly a goner. All our volunteer firefighters could do was see to it that the surrounding buildings were saved. Somewhere in the cloud of smoke was Satch.

Putting out fires was Satch Lusk's life. He was the only full-time fireman in Haskell, so that made him the Chief. He and his wife lived above the fire station in a simple apartment. By the time I was old enough to remember him, his children were grown and had moved from Haskell. Mrs. Lusk was one of the women who babysat me, and that meant I occasionally got to spend an evening in their home above the station. Satch Lusk was the person I wanted to grow up and be like during my "I'm going to be a fireman" stage.

One of my happiest memories to this day is that of dad taking me down to the fire station on Saturday mornings, so I could play on the trucks. I think we had an inside track with Satch, because I don't remember any of the other boys or girls doing it. He was usually there to give me a fire hat to wear while I pretended to race off to towering infernos. And once in a while, he and I actually took the truck out for a run around the block.

As I grew older, I learned more about Satch Lusk. I learned that in addition to being a quiet man and my friend, he was the one person in Haskell who risked his life more than any other. Every time the fire whistle blew, Satch was the first one to arrive on the scene. He would hook up the hose and get the pumper working, and he would be putting water on the fire when the first wave of volunteers arrived. Sometimes, he would be the only one there to break through a door to make sure no one was trapped inside.

If you had seen him, you'd never have guessed he was the Fire Chief. He was thin as a rail, and he looked like one gust of wind would blow him over. But he had more courage than any Hollywood character will ever have. When I think of the real heroes I have known, Satch Lusk is at the top of my list.

22

Movin' On

In Haskell, the funeral home had more prestige than the Chamber of Commerce. That's because more people were leaving town than coming into it. Bill Holden was the owner of (yes, you guessed it) Holden's Funeral Home. He had inherited the business from his father. The Holdens were one of Haskell's founding families. The original mortuary had been located on the West side of the Square. The new funeral home was one block North of the Square, just across the street from the Piggly Wiggly grocery store.

When I was a child, I was scared to death of Bill Holden. His daughter, Millie, and I were friends, and that meant we would play at each other's houses. I always prayed that Bill wouldn't be at home when I went to her house. But my prayers were not always answered. Bill Holden looked like a funeral director. He'd be the person you'd pick out of a lineup when asked to choose "the undertaker." When I grew up, I discovered he was actually a very nice man. I'm just telling you how he struck me before I was five.

There were always stories circulating about the funeral home, but the one I'm going to tell you took "first prize" in those days. It actually happened; I saw the evidence with my own eyes. Bill had recently hired an employee—a kind of handy-man around the funeral home—the person who was on duty at night. This also meant the man drove the ambulance after hours, rushing persons to our local hospital, or bringing them back to the funeral home if a trip to the hospital was unnecessary.

One particular night, there was a "killin" in Haskell. It fell the man's lot to go with Bill Holden to the murder scene and bring the deceased back to the funeral home. I don't understand everything that happened next. But I'm told that sometimes, after a violent death, a body will have a spasm. Well, that's what happened as Bill and his assistant were wheeling the corpse inside. Seems the old boy just sort of "sat up." The assistant, unfamiliar with things like that, thought he was witnessing a genuine resurrection—or something worse. Instead of hanging around for the whole show, he turned and ran through a door out into the night.

When I say that he ran through a door, I mean he ran *through* a door. He didn't even bother to open it, and Bill said he never even broke stride! When I heard the story the next day, I didn't believe it. So, I asked dad to take me down to the funeral home and see for myself. Sure enough, the door was broken off its hinges, lying on the floor of the attached garage where the hearse was parked. And as I understand it, the assistant was never seen in town again. He didn't even come back to get his last paycheck.

23

The Badge

Law enforcement in Haskell was in the hands of three principal persons: Frank Jircaick, "Bull" Barnett, and Garth Garrett. Frank was our Texas Highway Patrolman. "Bull" was the city Police Chief, and Garth was the County Sheriff. Garth's nickname was "tangle eye," because he was severely cross-eyed. I wouldn't tell you that, except it's important for this story.

Garth Garrett had succeeded Bill Pennington as County Sheriff when I was in elementary school. He was still serving in the office when I left for college. Each time he came up for re-election, the fine people of Haskell had the good sense to keep him on the job. He had their respect—and mine. Together with Frank and "Bull," he kept Haskell safe enough to walk alone, anytime, anywhere. I never had to do official business with

Garth (I did with "Bull"), but I do remember a few times when I hoped he was not around.

Garth didn't look like any of the police officers on television today. He was short and heavyset. He nearly always had a big plug of chewing tobacco between his cheek and gum. His hat looked like it was older than he was, but he'd worn it enough that it "fit." And there, on his right side, was a pistol that impressed anyone who saw it—a real Texas side arm.

I have two clear memories of Garth Garrett. The first one is of the night he broke up a fight in front of the Texas Café. Word had it that he moved right into the fray and had the two offenders at bay in no time. I saw him shortly after the incident, and I remember looking at him the way someone might have looked at Matt Dillon after he'd cleaned out the riffraff in the Long Branch Saloon.

The second memory is legend. It circulated around Haskell for years; it may still be making the rounds for all I know. Seems a crime had been committed, but no one could tell exactly where it happened. A witness to the whole event said he saw Garth responding to the call, running down the street as fast as he could go—heading north, but looking south!

Haskell didn't have many legends, much less legends in their own time. Garth Garrett came close.

24

Soldier of Mis-Fortune

Bobby Black and I received our Eagle Scout awards the same night at the Methodist Church in Haskell. He was one year older, and we were not close friends. But we made the Scouting journey together, and we played Little League Baseball. I was a Ram; he was a Tiger. Beyond that, we didn't have a lot in common.

Most of us thought that Bobby was "strange." He was not excessive, just unusual. For instance, one day in Mr. McCoy's physics' class, he put his mouth on the gas jet, filled it up, took out a cigarette lighter, and shot a stream of flame across the room. He was always the one who'd take a dare, and on that score he was the undisputed champion. But because he was unpredictable, a lot of kids kept their distance.

After graduation from high school, I lost track of Bobby. In fact, it was years before I thought of him. It was only when dad told me that Bobby was on death row in Huntsville. His trial was notorious in Texas. He was found guilty of murdering his wife. He had taken out an ad in *Soldier of Fortune* magazine, seeking someone to do the job. Someone did. But Bobby was ruled to have been the murderer. It was a controversial case that stunned everyone in Haskell.

By the time I knew all this, Bobby had served for years in the penitentiary, but his time was running out. One time, when I was near Huntsville, I tried to get in to see him. But it was more complicated than I had figured, and I didn't make it. I wrote him a note, but I never heard from him. Not long after, he was executed. He is still the only person I've ever known personally to have been on death row, and executed there.

Bobby's death hit me much harder than I thought it would, and even years later, I find myself thinking about him. At the oddest moments, memories will come flooding back. Memories of baseball games, camping trips, and school days. Memories of how often we used to say that Bobby was "different," even if in a likeable sort of way. I guess we didn't know how different. And we surely didn't know what was brewing behind those unusual acts to get attention.

We were never able to get behind his gold-toothed smile, to what might have been—even then—a hurting heart. Bobby wouldn't let us in. Even if he would have, it's hard to say what a group of teenagers could have said or done to make any difference. It's always easier to ignore "the weird kids" than it is to find out why they are the way they are. We liked Bobby, but we liked him at a distance that both he and we had created.

Bobby was my first reminder that someone can be standing right beside you on the night when the awards are handed out; someone who is hurting real bad on the inside. Someone can be in the seat next to yours on the plane; someone whose life is falling apart. The world is full of soldiers of misfortune.

25

A Hard-Working Man

Chances are, the first time you saw Olin Bartlett, you would only see part of him. The hidden part would be under a car, sticking out of a sink cabinet, or down a manhole. Olin was Haskell's version of "Mr. Fixit." He was either the first person you'd call for help—or the last. But whenever he showed up, you knew he could do it. I don't remember hearing anyone ever say he'd failed to fix something. I do remember some folks reporting that he might have a few parts left over after the repair job. But no matter, they weren't necessary.

Olin ran his operation out of a little shop beside his house. He usually had two or three cars jacked up, in various stages of repair. Inside, there was no telling what you'd find. People brought him every imaginable motor, appliance, and gadget. We took our Philco radio to him once. Olin just seemed to "know" how to get things going again.

In addition to his repair skills, he was Satch Lusk's right-hand man on the fire department. When they were together, they looked like Andy Griffith and Barney Fife. Olin was the only guy I knew who had a siren in his car as a volunteer firefighter, and he would turn it on when he was responding to a call.

On hot summer nights in Haskell, you'd almost certainly find Olin umpiring a Little League baseball game. In the daytime, it was not unusual for him to come to your house just to see if there was anything that needed fixin' or to make sure something he had recently repaired was still working. If something he fixed ever did quit, he would never charge you to fix it again. Olin was his own guarantee.

Later on, Olin went to work for the City of Haskell. He was the superintendent of streets and water. That meant long hours of lifting, twisting, digging, and pulling. It also meant driving every kind of maintenance equipment the city owned. Olin considered it his duty to keep Haskell running. Most of us will never know how much he did and how many things kept working because Olin was on the job.

One day, inside his shop, Olin simply dropped dead. They found him a few hours later. But I'm sure that by then, he had already passed through the Pearly Gates, no doubt asking St. Peter, "You got anything up here that needs fixin'?"

26

Great Physicians

When I travel to other cities, I like to read a local newspaper. You can learn a lot about a place by doing that. On one such trip, I came across an advertisement for a group of physicians whose claim to fame was that they made house calls. I think they called themselves, "Doctors At Your Door" or something like that.

As I read the ad, I realized how much times have changed. What doctors today use as a major selling point for their practices was standard operating procedure for physicians in Haskell in the fifties. Every doctor made house calls. No big deal. An ad in The Haskell Free Press for "Doctors At Your Door" wouldn't have evoked a yawn back then, much less a phone call.

In Haskell, sooner or later, you used all the doctors: Dr. Williams, Dr. Thigpen, Dr. Kimbrough, Dr. Cadenhead, and (a little later) Dr. Colbert. When you went to the Haskell Clinic, you could wait to see your "main doctor" if you wanted to, but often you'd take the next-available one. Dr. Thigpen was our customary family physician, but growing up, I went to every one of the doctors I've named above. But it was Dr. Thigpen who made most of the house calls to our home.

During my first-grade year, I missed a lot of school due to a strep infection and tonsillitis. Dr. Thigpen made a fair share of house calls during those days. I was never in the running for being his best patient. More likely, he remembers me as "the little demon" who fought him, ran from him, and kicked him whenever the word "shot" was spoken.

I especially remember one house call. I kicked and screamed so much that he finally gave up and left. About a half-hour later, he was back. He came into my room, not carrying his usual black bag, but holding a large, blue fighter jet—the very one I had been coveting at the Haskell Pharmacy. He handed it to me and said, "This is for you." Then, he left.

"Doctors At Your Door." I'm not all that impressed. I've known doctors who came to your door because they really cared—really loved you, and they proved it with big blue fighter jets.

27

The River of No Return

Paul Harvey is as well known for his series "The Rest of the Story" as he is for his radio newscasts. He has a unique way of adding here-to-fore unknown information to the lives of famous people. I have a "rest of the story" about Dr. Thigpen. You need to know about it.

After several months of trying to cure my strep throat and tonsillitis, not to mention all the verbal and physical abuse I dished out to him during that time, Dr. Thigpen announced to my parents that the only thing he knew to do was remove my tonsils. A date was set. Dr. Ernest Kimbrough was recruited to be the surgeon; Dr. Thigpen would be the anesthesiologist.

When I learned of my "fate worse than death," I made Dr. Thigpen promise that he would sing me a song while he was putting me to sleep on the operating table. He agreed to my demand; he probably would have agreed to almost anything just to get that operation over with. He even threw in a tour of the operating room and the room where I would be staying when the surgery was over.

Dr. Thigpen gave my parents the choice of either Tuesday or Thursday for the operation. I voted for Thursday; they and Dr. Thigpen voted for Tuesday. I never heard if Dr. Kimbrough voted. I lost 3 to 1. When Tuesday rolled around, we got up early and drove out to Haskell County Hospital. Mom and dad checked me into the room, the nurse put the backless hospital gown on me, and she gave me a red pill that was supposed to make me drowsy. It didn't.

I knew my options were running out. When Dr. Kimbrough came into the room, I did my best to convince him that Thursday was really the best day for the surgery. I was holding out hope that since he was the surgeon, and hadn't voted originally, I might still have a chance of winning him over to my side. I told him I would be happy to come back on Thursday. He called dad and mom out of the room and as dad later told me, he seriously considered postponing the operation. He was afraid I was too upset.

Dr. Thigpen walked up and squelched the whole idea. In effect, he said, "No way! We've gotten him this far; we're not turning back now." He had the scars to prove the battle had been hard fought. The operation went on as scheduled. And Dr. Thigpen kept his word. As he dropped ether onto the little mask that covered my nose and mouth, sending me into a deep sleep, he sang to me. It was only years later that dad got up the courage to tell me what he sang. As I drifted into la-la land, the only song that came to Dr. Thigpen's mind was the theme song from the movie, "The River of No Return."

28

Meeting Dandy Don

I don't remember how young I was when dad and I began making trips to Fort Worth and Dallas to see ballgames. In the summer, it was baseball with the Fort Worth Cats. In the fall, it was football with the Mustangs at Southern Methodist University.

Our routine was the same. We'd leave Haskell in time to get to Fort Worth for lunch or dinner at Cattleman's Steak House. If we were going to see the Cats, we'd be sure and finish eating in time to get to the ballpark to see their batting practice. If we were going to see the Mustangs, we liked to get there to see their warm-ups.

After the game, we'd hang around the dugout or locker room, waiting for the players to come out, so we could get a few autographs. Then, we'd head for home. If it was an afternoon game, we'd talk about it all the way back to Haskell. If it was a night game, I'd bed down in the back seat, and dad would drive well past midnight. My next memory would be waking up in my own bed. It's a parent-thing to be able to pick you up and take you into the house without waking you up.

By the time I began elementary school—or maybe it was early junior high—the Cats had folded, but the Mustangs were still "hot." They were led by quarterback Don Meredith. "Number 17" was breaking Southwest Conference records right and left. He was the brightest star in the SMU football sky since Doak Walker.

In Haskell, I *was* Don Meredith. I put "17" in black Crayola on both sides of my red Hutch helmet, and (by my own decree) I was the only person allowed to use that number or go by the name "Dandy Don." When the gang assembled in Bill

Perry's front yard for a Saturday game, I called plays and imagined myself executing them with the same finesse that Meredith had with the Mustangs week after week. No doubt about it, I was Don Meredith whenever the "Avenue H Mustangs" took the field.

In Don's senior year at SMU, dad and I decided to go to two games, instead of our usual one. The first one was an evening game played at the Cotton Bowl, the location of SMU football home games at that time. And like always, we waited by the locker room after the game, hoping for glimpses of some of the players—especially "Dandy Don."

And that's when it happened. As we stood there, a man dressed in a suit walked up and asked me, "Who are you waiting for?" Even though the man was a stranger, I was not hesitant to answer, "Don Meredith," and held up the program and pen I had in my hand, awaiting his autograph. "Well," the man continued,

"I'm his father, and this is his mother," pointing at the well-dressed woman standing nearby.

Now, let me be clear. Being from Haskell did not make you a cultural connoisseur, but it didn't mean you fell off the back of a truck either. So, both dad and I were initially skeptical. But we were too polite to say so. Nevertheless, the looks on our faces must have given us away, because the stranger continued, "Would you like to meet Don?"

Would I like to meet Don? Is the Pope Catholic? In an instant, I responded, "Sure!" still not certain the man was legitimate or this was really happening. But 30 seconds and 50 feet later, there we were—in the SMU locker room—talking with Don Meredith. He had just stepped out of the shower, and he greeted me with a wet handshake and a towel wrapped around his waist. But who cares? I had touched and actually spoken with Don Meredith! And I knew his parents!

In that brief visit, we made plans to see the three of them after Don's final game with the Mustangs—a game with the TCU Horned Frogs, played in Fort Worth. I lived for that day, and I think I played the best front-yard football in my life in the weeks leading up to it. I was the only kid in Haskell who had met Don Meredith and his parents. No one could top that!

When the big day came, we drove to Fort Worth. The weather was not our friend, and it's not an exaggeration to say we "froze solid" as we hovered under a blanket in the stadium, watching Don Meredith play his final game for SMU. Dad and I had no idea if the Merediths would remember our plan, but when we made our way outside the locker room, there they were—this time with Don's fiancé. When Don came out, we had another brief visit and went our separate ways.

I figured that was it. But about a week later, I received a postcard from Don in the mail. On one side was his picture, posed in a position indicating he was on the verge of throwing one of those passes he was famous for. On the other side, was a short, hand-written note that read, "Glad to have met you, Steve. I hope you play for the Mustangs some day. Don."

Cloud Nine? Shoot, no! I passed right through it while on my way to Cloud 99!

29

Woody

If you stand on the front steps of Haskell High School today and look across the street, you're looking at what used to be Woody's. You'll see a sign that reads, "Administration Building." But if you lived in Haskell in the fifties and sixties, you'll know you're looking at Woody's. Sometime after that, the school district bought the building to use as its headquarters.

No matter what color they paint the building or what signs they put up on it, you'll never see anything other than Woody's. This was the lunchtime hangout and after-hours gathering place for nearly everyone who ever lived and went to school in Haskell. Woody Frazier owned and operated the place (along with his wife and student employees), and it was our version of the "Happy Day's" drive in.

Actually, there was an earlier model of Woody's before the one I frequented in high school. A picture of the original hung in the "new" building, and Woody's ad in each year's annual preserved a picture of it as well. I have some fleeting memories of going in the first one when I was a little kid. But Woody's was mostly reserved for teenagers in junior and senior high. The original Woody's didn't burn down; it just wore out.

There was nothing special about the food at Woody's. You can only do so much with hamburgers and french fries. Other places served up equally-good fare, but none of them could compare with Woody's. For one thing, you could order something called a "Super Dog," which was similar to today's corn dog on a stick, except it wasn't made of corn meal. It was more of a dough batter, with just the slightest hint of sweetness. Other than that, Woody served up standard stuff.

What made Woody's special…was Woody. You went there to talk to him as much as to eat his food. Except for the rare times when he wasn't in the building, Woody was your host from the time you walked through the door until you left. He knew everyone by name, and he always made you feel you had just come home. He worked the counter in his white short-sleeved shirt, with a white apron that tied around his neck and waist. He kept a small pencil behind his left ear and a green pad on the counter to write down your order. If things were not real busy, he'd deliver the food himself, right to your table, and sit down to visit while you ate.

The noon hour at Woody's was something to behold. A tidal wave of kids would pour out of the school and crash through the door of the diner. They would shout orders in a way that only a wizard could have followed and filled. Woody and his food team had piles of burgers, Super Dogs, and fries waiting, and the whole thing went much smoother than you would have expected. Unless you were one of the early arrivers, it was useless to think about getting a table. And even if you did, you could barely hear yourself speak because of the din of noisy customers and the music coming from the jukebox. But it didn't matter. The same "Woody spirit" pervaded the atmosphere.

I had been gone from Haskell for a while, when one day I heard that Woody had closed his drive in and sold it to the school district. I felt a wave of sadness wash over me when I realized Woody's was no more. I grieved partly for myself, but also for the students yet to come, who would never get to experience the place and the person. I grieved for those who would stand on the school steps, look across the street, and only see an administration building.

For a while, Woody came back into service in Haskell and managed the new Dairy Queen. It gave some of us the chance to see him when we were back in town. No visit to Haskell was ever complete if you didn't stop by to see Woody. He still greeted us by name and made us feel special. But it wasn't the same, and we knew it; Woody knew it too. After a while, even Woody had to go back into retirement; even Woody's get old—and die. But there's one thing Woody will never be, and that's forgotten by those of us who used to race across the school yard every day at noon just to see him and eat his food.

30

Kindergarten Dropout

When my parents bought their dream home at 500 South Avenue H in Haskell, they had no idea plans were in the works for the city to build a new elementary school on land catty-cornered to our property. To a child growing up in Haskell in the early '50's that was like having Disney World going up next door. The silver paint on the swings, seesaws, slides, and monkey bars was barely dry before I was trying them out. And when school ended each day, that playground was "mine, all mine."

But as the world turns, that magic kingdom became a school I was supposed to attend. The year was 1953, and the thing was called "Kindergarten." Back then in Texas, it was not required, but it was assumed you'd go. Mothers considered

119

kindergarten an answer to prayer. As the summer of 1953 drew to a close, Jerre Sue Couch and I (the two eligible candidates on the block) began to set our sights on spending our mornings in kindergarten.

Mom and I met the teacher on visitation day, and she gave us the list of items each student was expected to have. I took my list to the Haskell Pharmacy and Perry Brothers to get my supplies: large pencil with an equally-big eraser, Big Chief tablet, blunt-end scissors, Crayolas, and edible paste (yes, you read that last item correctly). Everything had to go into some kind of carrier. I chose the Lone Ranger satchel. It looked like a Western-style, cloth briefcase—complete with a plastic picture of the old L.R. on the front side. Combined with my Roy Rogers lunch box, I was ready to go. Tomorrow, I would become a bonafide kindergarten student.

Tomorrow came----early. I got up, ate breakfast, and gathered my stuff. I knew Jerre Sue was getting ready too. But suddenly, something happened. Several hundred invisible Indians showed up at my bedroom window asking, "Who's going to fight us while you're in kindergarten?" The green, plastic Army men in the cigar box called out to me, "Who's going to command our next raid?" My stick horse neighed in the corner as if to say, "Who's going to ride me while you're gone?"

I stood still, stunned by all the voices speaking to me. And in that moment, I laid down my Lone Ranger satchel and my Roy Rogers lunch box, and became the only kindergarten dropout I've ever known.

31

First Kiss

I don't remember when I first learned about kissing—I mean boy/girl kissing, not the kissing you got from your parents and grandparents. I probably learned about it from watching mom and dad. I certainly didn't learn about it (and other things) like kids do today, while watching television or surfing the web. I knew about kissing before I had ever seen television, and what I knew interested me.

I signed up for "Kissing Lab" early in my first-grade year. It was held during pallet time in the "Little House in the Back of the Room." Pallet time came right after lunch. Mrs. Stubblefield made us all lie down on our pallets and play "the Quiet Game." Often, Mrs. Stubblefield used pallet time as an occasion to leave the room, probably to go down to the principal's office and look for loopholes in her teaching contract.

The "Little House in the Back of the Room" was used for various educational activities, skits, games, etc. But it was also the location of "Kissing Lab," and when Mrs. Stubblefield left the room, lab was in session. The length lab time lasted was directly related to how long she was gone. Sometimes more than one couple could experiment; at other times (especially if the experiment was long), only one couple made it to the lab and back to their respective pallets.

Now, let's be clear. Kissing was not something you rushed into. Kissing lab was the culmination of a long, evolving process. It started with talk, lots of talk—usually among the boys—though I now suspect the girls were talking about it too. A lot of factors went into the decision. Questions like, "Who are you going to kiss?" and "How are you going to kiss?" had to be thoroughly discussed. People who omitted this phase were not considered "cool," although later on in high school they did seem to end up dating the prettiest girls. Nevertheless, the rules for lab were fixed in first grade, and talking was clearly step one.

It was a great day when a boy decided which girl he would kiss. We probably celebrated the decision for days, and during this time we entered the phase of note passing—not to the girl, but to someone who was willing to find out if "she likes you." Sometimes the messenger returned with an inconclusive report, and you had to eventually take matters into your own hands, acting on your best-available evidence. Besides, it could change from day to day, maybe even hour to hour. In the final analysis, you simply had to "go for it."

That meant deciding to go to the lab with the girl you'd chosen. Again, someone else usually did the asking and returned to say she would agree to go. It would be about six years later before we cut out the middle-man. In first grade the actual invitation was usually extended during recess, because you were not allowed to talk during pallet time. Plans had to be made somewhere, and the playground was the port of entry into "Kissing Lab."

I chose Donna Ruth Sanders. The above steps in the process had confirmed that she was my best bet—and—glory of glories, she had agreed to go with me to "The Little House in the Back of the Room" during pallet time that afternoon. I don't remember much between recess and pallet time. Life was a hormonal blur, even though none of us actually knew what hormones were. I walked around in a daze.

But I'll never forget the actual experience of my first kiss. At the appointed time, Donna Ruth and I slipped off our pallets and made our way to, and inside, "The Little House in the Back of the Room." At first, no one did anything. But I knew the first move was mine. So....with time standing still....I moved closer to her, leaned in, puckered my lips....and....kissed her. In what seemed like an instant after experiencing my first kiss, Donna Ruth raised her hand, and slapped my face off.

32

Respect

My hat is perpetually off in honor any man or woman who chooses public-school teaching as a career. They are the ones who should make millions of dollars a year, not jocks who throw, dribble, hit, and run. The public-school teacher takes more heat for less pay than any other professional. Very few get the respect they deserve from either students or parents.

It wasn't that way growing up in Haskell in the fifties. Respect for teachers wasn't even up for a vote. It was etched in stone. Pre-schoolers were prepared by their parents with a barrage of "obey your teacher" comments. Kids in school scared us spitless with their stories of what teachers did there. I swear that every first-grader believed there was an electric paddle with a nail in it at the principal's office. Offenders were taken into a little room, and the paddle was turned on. Teachers left the room, abandoning you to a fate worse than death. Respect? You better believe it!

My first-grade teacher was Mrs. Stubblefield. She was the human incarnation of Mamma Bear. I began to wonder if what I'd heard was true. I began to suspect my fears were unfounded. Then, I hit second grade with Mrs. Fagan. Children prayed not to be put into her class. My prayer evidently slipped past God. She was at the other end of the spectrum from Mrs. Stubblefield.

Through the eyes of an eight-year-old, Mrs. Fagan was old—and mean. I'm sure neither was true, but it sure seemed like it at the time. We figured she had gone into teaching after a long stint as a Marine Drill Sergeant. Respect? You better believe it! In fact, it's hard to over-exaggerate how much respect we had for her. I can illustrate it this way. Mrs. Fagan allowed us to have two bathroom "trips" per day, not counting lunch time and recess. I think students who rode the bus were allowed to "go" before getting on the bus to head for home. The bus drivers made that rule, not Mrs. Fagan.

So fixed were these bathroom laws that one of my best friends (I don't have the heart to tell you his name) came to school one day feeling queasy, doubting that the legislated "trips" would be sufficient. And sure enough, they weren't. Even though his mother had written Mrs. Fagan a note, he didn't have the courage to show it to her. It wasn't long before his potty privileges were exhausted, but his needs were not. And there were not enough lunch and recess breaks to make up the difference.

I swear the rest of this story is true, although my friend didn't tell me about it until many years later when we came back to Haskell for a high school homecoming. When his next crisis "hit," he faced his moment of decision. Should he tell Mrs. Fagan and enter a world into which no one had gone before, or should he sit on it, literally? My friend chose the second option. Respect? We had it!

33

Be My Valentine

Everyone looked forward to celebrating Valentine's Day in elementary school. We didn't dismiss school for it; we observed it right in the classroom, which added to the fun. Home-room mothers were called in for special duty on that day. Together with teachers, they provided special treats and activities. I remember Red Hots and little heart-shaped candies with phrases like "Be My Valentine" on them. All these things were fine, but everyone knew they were just the preliminaries. The whole day was designed to build toward "the Great Valentine's Day Card Exchange."

Step One in this sacred process was the preparation of mail pouches. We worked on them days in advance, decorating them with crayon and construction-paper designs. Each student's name was written in large letters at the top of each pouch. Even kids who didn't like art seemed to get into it for Valentine's Day, much more than when we made Pilgrim hats and turkeys at Thanksgiving. Your mail pouch was your "personal statement."

When the pouches were completed, we hung them face high all around the room. Like baby birds waiting to be fed, each pouch's mouth gaped open in anticipation. Everyone knew that their pouch would soon be filled to the brim with all sorts of cards. Valentine's Day at school was a day when no one was left out. Everyone was loved and remembered, with cards of all shapes and sizes.

And that was Step Two in this phenomenon—the selection of the cards themselves. Every pharmacy and dime store in Haskell stocked up with Valentine cards. You didn't have to worry about the town running short on them. But the trick was to get to stores early enough before they had been picked over. It was important to select cards that reflected your spirit and style.

Most of the cards came in plastic bags, usually holding enough for every person in your class. Some were simply cards. No envelopes, just little cards with cute characters and short phrases ("I like you, Valentine") on them. The cards had enough blank space to write your name, but not much more. You didn't need to address these, because you would go around the room and drop them randomly into each pouch. On Valentine's Day, everyone was your friend.

In each bag there were a few larger cards, with envelopes. You could address them to the people you considered your friends on a year-round basis, not just on Valentine's Day. These cards usually had tabs on them, so your friends could stand them up at home, remembering that your friendship was "a notch above" the generic cards. The messages were more elaborate ("I like you a lot, Valentine"), and the blank space was a little bigger, so you could write your name larger. Often, people wrote notes on the backs of these cards. And one of them was designed for your teacher.

Then there was Step Three. There were individual cards for sale, cards not in the bag—that "special card" for that "special person" in your class, in your life. No card factory could ever successfully second-guess that kind of card and dump it into a bag. That card had to be purchased separately from the more-expensive card section. That card was chosen only after stillness that resembled worship, and almost always not the first card you looked at. For a moment, elementary school was not a "child" thing; it was a door leading into a future of heart-felt relationships. Valentine's Day was a forecast of things to come.

What never varied was the moment when the pouches were taken off the wall and carried back to each seat for inspection. We sorted the cards into categories that matched the description of cards I've noted above. Every card mattered, but as you sorted them into their respective stacks, you were really waiting and watching to see if "someone" had put the "special card" into your pouch. In fact, you had to be looking for this card, because if another kid saw it before you did, he or she would grab it, run around shouting something embarrassing, and (God forbid) even read the card out loud. So, when you saw the card in the pouch, you immediately put it into a secret place for later.

I liked to alphabetize my cards and read them in order, carefully checking each one for any messages hand-written on the back. I also separated the cards with tabs, so I could stand them up in my room that evening. But nothing compared to that "moment"—usually at home alone in my room—when I opened that "special card," sniffed for any evidence of perfume, and then read (and re-read) the message inside. Ah, sweet love!

34

Annuals

One way to measure time during the school year in Haskell was the span between the day school annuals were ordered and the day when they came in. That meant about six months, roughly the period from October to April. In fact, it was easy to forget they had been ordered at all, which made it even better. One day, when you least expected it, the principal would announce, "The annuals are here."

That meant Annual Day was not far away. On that great day we assembled in the cafeteria or auditorium, lining up to get our annuals. There were two lines: one for those who had ordered their annuals with their names printed on the cover, and one for those who hadn't. Either way, you got your annual in alphabetical order. When every student had an annual, step one was completed.

Step two was for everyone to sit down for a couple of minutes, flipping through your annual to be sure there were no blank pages. Defective annuals could be returned for a good one, if they had not been "written in." Step two also included smelling that combination odor of printed pages and annual covers that cannot be found anywhere else in the world. But you had to be discreet; it wasn't cool to be seen sniffing your annual.

Step three was bedlam. For the rest of the afternoon, we circulated around the room signing each other's annuals. This step had at least three phases in it. Phase one was signing every picture of yourself in the annual. This step ruined any hope that people could be recognized years later. There's something about adolescent hormones that demand signatures be written over the face. Even now, I try to stare through the ballpoint pen ink trying to remember who those people were, and what they looked like.

Phase two of the third step was what I call the "short note period." You were allowed to write them in the advertisement section of the annual, around the margins of the pages. Here is where you could record the "You are going to go far" and "To a really nice boy/girl" comments. People you didn't know real well were allowed to write in this section, as well as your circle of general friends. This section of the annual was the place to resurrect generic memories (and a few secret messages), and to wonder, "Where are they now?"

Phase three of step three was for "that certain person." He or she was given a whole page to write on. This page would not be written on during Annual Day. In fact, it was probably not written in public, much less read there. Annuals would be exchanged, taken home, and written in there. Time seemed to stand still while you waited for your annual to be given back, and the other person's to be returned. Even when the returns were completed, we hesitated to open the annual to see what had been written. You hoped the words would preserve forever your deepest feelings, and keep alive your promised future. And most of all, you could only hope that at next year's Annual Day, the same person would write on that special page again.

35

Driver's Ed

The summer before your sixteenth birthday meant one thing in Haskell—Driver's Education. It also meant one of the high school coaches could pick up some extra money teaching it. Coach Middleton was my instructor. Every morning for four weeks, we went to the parking lot behind the administration building for our training.

We began with some classroom instruction. We were each given a Texas Drivers' License Handbook, which is not the most exciting summertime reading for teenagers. We went over the rules and regulations until we could almost say them in our sleep. We took practice written tests and broke up into pairs to drill each other on the fine points of obeying the laws of the road.

With the "book learning" under our belts, we spent the rest of our time behind the wheel. Haskell High School had two worn-out vehicles at our disposal. In those days you had to be able to drive standard shift and automatic transmission automobiles. The standard shift was a regular car. The automatic transmission vehicle was a station wagon. We alternated days between the two, putting them through planned and unexpected twists and turns, stops and starts, and other maneuvers required to get the license. For most of us, parallel parking was the ultimate challenge. Some of us came right up to the official testing day unsure as to how that part of the exam would turn out.

The most fun was on the street between the back of the administration building and the gymnasium. Coach Middleton would stand about three quarters of the way down the street. He would motion for us to head in his direction. When we were close enough to hear him, he would shout, "Stop! We were supposed to hit the brakes as quickly as possible, so Coach could calculate our reaction time with his stopwatch. This procedure also taught us how far a car would really go after you applied the brakes. We were beginning to learn that we were handling a machine that was a lot more powerful than we were.

But all this was in anticipation of the day when Coach Middleton would let us take a car out on the highway. He never told us exactly when that would happen; I'm guessing it was whenever he sized up the group's prowess and decided his life was no longer in jeopardy. We usually took the station wagon, because seven of us could pack into it, in addition to Coach Middleton. That meant three of us were in the section behind the backseat—something I'm sure no one is allowed to do today. For an hour or so, we would rotate drivers and get the feel of the open road. We learned to maintain our speed, determine when it was safe to pass, and other skills different from in-town driving.

Larry was in my group. And on the day in question, Larry was at the wheel. We were heading back into town so another group could use the car. It had been a good day. Far in the distance, there was a house on the left side of the road, a mailbox across from it on the right side, and a dog not far from the mailbox. "Watch out for the dog," Coach said as we got closer. "Okay," replied Larry.

As we approached, the old dog noticed us. And as he had done a thousand times before, he began to amble across the road toward the house. No problem for the dog…or for us. Plenty of room. "Slow down," Coach said, " let the dog get across." No answer from Larry. Only forward progress and a strange silence in the station wagon.

Wouldn't it be great to know what happens in the brain sometimes? Rod Serling knew, I think. "Twilight Zone" was proof that strange things can happen in the old noggin. And all I know, from this point of the story on, is that we all had a "Twilight Zone" experience. Instead of slowing down, Larry speeded up. "I said slow down." Coach spoke with a little more emphasis. Still nothing from Larry. At this point, the old dog realized he was in trouble. He increased his pace and made it to the left lane of the Farm-to-Market Road. Larry followed him, almost expertly lining up the hood ornament on the station wagon right between the dog's eyes. Coach tried one last time, "Larry, for God's sake, slow down!"

Bang! Larry hit the dog "dead on" and only hit the brakes after we heard the sound of the impact. We skidded to a stop and then backed up. The dog was deader than a hammer. All Coach could do was say Larry's name over and over. He got out of the station wagon, walked up to the nearby house, and knocked on the door. At least one good thing—the dog didn't belong to the woman at the door. Seems the old fella was a stray that had been wandering around the place for a while. Like most farm families, they had fed the dog, but they didn't know who it belonged to. Someone probably dropped the dog off on the side of the road. That kind of thing happened.

But we couldn't leave the dog in the road. The farmer gave us a burlap sack that was large enough to stuff the dog into it. We wrapped him up the best we could, drove down a side dirt road, and had our version of a "burial at sea" as we tossed the remains into a bar ditch.

Larry passed Driver's Ed along with the rest of us. But I don't remember him driving a lot.

36

Separate, But Equal

Growing up in Haskell in the fifties and early sixties was to live there when "separate, but equal" was the law. It referred to the segregation of blacks and whites into different school systems. The law permitted the separation as long as the two facilities and programs were "separate, but equal." The law remained in effect until my sophomore year in 1963, when it (and other laws like it around the country) were declared unconstitutional.

I got my driver's license the Fall of my sophomore year. One of the first places I drove was to that part of Haskell everyone called "Colored Town." For some reason, I wanted to see the former black school. I wanted to see where the new students in our school had gone before integration came to town.

I was not prepared for what I saw. I didn't even have to get out of the car to know "separate, but equal" didn't apply. The building was run down all over. When I went inside, I entered through a door that led into the combination cafeteria/auditorium. The lunch tables and chairs were dilapidated. The curtain on stage, where plays were no doubt performed, was in shreds. The building had an odor I now recognize in places that have been declared unsafe or health hazards. But for my life up to that time, the school had been just fine—"separate, but equal."

I don't remember anything else from that visit. But I'll never forget the emotions that welled up in me that afternoon. It was my first unprotected exposure to a form of racism that, while non-violent, was just as demeaning as a fire hose or police dog ever was. It was a way of life all of us—whites and blacks alike—had come to accept, so much so that it was never even talked about. It was "just the way we lived" every day.

I can honestly say that my parents didn't raise me to be prejudiced toward people of other races. And that was true of the parents of all my friends, and almost all of the other people in Haskell. But in another way, that's what made the Haskell version of racism so bad. Nobody acknowledged it was there. Even the integration of the school system went off pretty much without a hitch. I guess there was something good about that.

But that day in the former black school building, I learned that racism doesn't have to be intentional. It can exist when no one even names it or acts as if it is there. Things remain "nice" so long as everyone understands the game and agrees to play. Walking back to my car that afternoon, I learned that "separate, but equal" was a lie.

37

A Real Christian

Church was important in Haskell in the fifties. For a town of under 4,000 residents, we had more than our share of congregations. I was put on the cradle roll at the First Methodist Church not long after I was born. My earliest memories include being at that church nearly every Sunday, and other times as well. Whether it was sitting with Mrs. Craft at the piano in kindergarten class or singing in the junior choir directed by Jo Cox, church was one of my "homes."

All this means that as far back as I can remember, I was a Christian. Being in church *was* being a Christian. And that's that. I was not Muslim, Hindu, or Jewish; I was a Christian. Besides, those other religions were not options in Haskell anyway. So, I was a Christian, or at least I thought so until the day the legitimacy of my "faith" was called into question.

It was Saturday. Riley Couch and I were playing "ice hockey" on roller skates on the sidewalk in front of my house. I must briefly digress to explain that last sentence. In Haskell, we played "ice hockey" on sidewalks, wearing roller skates. Needless to say, the rink was long, but not very wide. We used child-sized golf clubs (the kind we could buy at Perry Brothers 'dime store'), and the puck was half of a yo-yo. It was a two-person game. The object of the game (somewhat like real hockey) was to drive the puck past your opponent (not easy to do on a sidewalk) and shoot it over a designated crack near the end of the "rink."

Riley and I were in the middle of a match when his sister, Jerre Sue, walked over from her house. She had not come to watch us play hockey. She had come to speak with me about the state of my soul. She wasted no time in telling me, "You are not a Christian." Startled, I responded with a spirit of calm certainty, "Of course I am." "No, you are not," she retorted, "only Baptists are Christians, and you are not a Baptist." Well, friends...Methodists are known for generally taking a "live and let live" approach to things. We have our faith, but we realize that others do too. On a given day, that's okay. But there are limits. Being equated with Beelzebub is one of them.

I had not received any formal training in this sort of exchange, but I figured that if I raised my voice like she was raising hers—and if I raised it louder than hers—I could win by decibel default. I increased the volume of this unplanned theological controversy, and once again declared, "I am too a Christian!" Jerre Sue shot back, "No, you are not a Christian, because you are not a Baptist." Her tone made it clear she did not consider herself wrong or that she had any intention of losing this evangelistic debate. She was holding her ground with the confidence that "good always overcomes evil."

Well…when you cannot tell, you must show. Words must become deeds. Even Jesus said that. I concluded that my only option was to "prove" my faith by my works, honoring the theme of the Book of James and applying its message directly to Jerre Sue. So, I approached her and began to kick her shins with my roller skates. As she retreated, I continued to kick her, eventually driving her into our chainlink fence. As I did so, I yelled even louder (to reinforce the moment with both volume and heightened spirituality), "I am *too* a Christian! I am *too* a Christian!"

Somehow, Jerre Sue broke free and hobbled home on one leg grabbing her wounded shin with both hands. Riley had witnessed the whole controversy, and he was so overcome by it all that being a brother to Jerre Sue took precedence over being a friend to me. He ran home along with her. I was alone on the sidewalk. I kind of half slid, half skated my way into the house. The little I knew about Christianity seemed to teach against kicking someone in the shins with your roller skates into a chainlink fence. I could not think of a single verse in the Bible that taught this was an acceptable way to confirm your faith to those around you. There were no pictures of Jesus wearing roller skates in my Sunday School materials.

I went to my room. I cried. I repented of my sin. And I made God a promise that I have kept to this day. I promised God that if this kind of thing ever came up again, I would take my skates off first.

38

Outdoor Revivals

"Hot August nights" were the opening words of Neil Diamond's hit song, "Brother Love's Traveling Salvation Show." When the song made the Top 40, it was nothing new to me. Growing up in Haskell in the fifties, I was familiar with those nights. We referred to them as the annual "outdoor revival." The Methodists were not the only ones who had them, but ours are the ones I remember best.

Revival seating was comprised of wooden, folding chairs. Rows of them were set up between the church building and the parsonage. We did not typically include a tent, as some of the local churches did, but there was always a raised platform which the men in the church put together a week or so before the actual revival began. I think it was stored in one of the empty rooms in the church, which meant that they didn't have to start from scratch each year. It was large enough to include the preachers, choir, a piano taken from one of the Sunday School rooms, and an organ rented from a music store in Abilene. The platform was high enough so even those in the back row could see and hear what was going on up front.

The days leading up to the revival found the women busy on the telephone, lining up places for the visiting evangelist to eat at least two meals a day. This relieved the host family from having to feed the preacher as well, with the exception of breakfast. The women also made plans for the "dinner on the grounds," covered-dish supper that was held one evening during the revival. The other nights had to include assorted refreshments (definitely cold drinks), which were necessary elements of every revival in Haskell, especially those held during the hot, summer months.

I always looked forward to the annual outdoor revival. The congregation seemed more "alive" and "active" preceding and following it. Cooperation among the city's churches also increased. It was an unspoken rule that the local churches would dismiss their regular Sunday-evening services and attend any other church's revival service. That meant the largest attendance at the revival was usually on the first night. I'm sure the evangelist knew he was expected to preach really well at that service; the size of the crowd for the rest of the week would hinge on it.

Music also played a significant part in subsequent attendance. Some churches would bring in featured "song evangelists" in addition to the visiting preacher. We Methodists would include solos in the services from local folks, but the bulk of the music ministry fell upon the choir, which practiced "special numbers" for weeks leading up to the revival. We also had gospel hymnbooks which were only used during the revival. Each folding chair had one placed on it every night. Some of the congregational singing was planned (most likely to coincide with the evangelist's message), but the song leader would always solicit "favorites" from the crowd. This meant it was possible for the really popular songs to be sung every night.

The evening offering was also a big deal. For one thing, most churches only promised to give the visiting preacher (and any others brought in) a "love offering," which was a distribution of the total amount given during the revival. This solicitation could be very passionate and extended (especially if the money counters knew funds were not coming in at the expected clip), and when the ushers came forward to receive the evening offering, the organist and pianist were expected to team up for an inspiring and motivating duet.

But with all these things in place and done with great devotion, they were considered (and sometimes even called) "preliminaries" leading up to the sermon by the visiting clergyperson. He was invited from among a list of relatively well-known people, who "preached revivals." They might be full-time evangelists, or they could be pastors who had a reputation for evangelistic preaching. They were almost never first-timers. The annual revival was too important to entrust to rookies. Often, they were "returnees" who had preached for us before. The mere appearance of their names on the pre-revival publicity flyers would ignite the potential of larger attendance.

No matter when the sermon began, everyone settled in to an expectation that the evangelist would preach upwards of an hour—maybe more. Anything shorter than that put the whole service in jeopardy, and probably guaranteed the particular preacher would not be invited back again. He was supposed to be "wound up" and "prayed up." His only mission was to "lead us to the throne of grace," where Christians would re-dedicate themselves and non-Christians could be persuaded to "be saved" by accepting Jesus Christ as their personal Lord and Savior.

Under the inspiration of the Holy Spirit, the evangelist would preach from a biblical text that would accomplish these sacred aims, and probably be a message he had preached a number of times before. That was not a bad thing at all; a good sermon would only get better by preaching it more than once. Some visiting preachers were even known for their sermons, and when they brought out one of their "special messages," you could almost hear the crowd exude a collective sigh of anticipation.

As we sat in rapt attention, we used our revival songbooks for more than singing. They could be rolled up and used to swat mosquitoes, who also seemed to enjoy attending

160

the annual revival. The lights strung around the makeshift tabernacle were the plain, white variety (not the yellow insect-repelling type), and the longer the service went and the more people sweated (due to heat and spiritual engagement), the more mosquitoes you could expect to show up. Even on nights when the mosquitoes decided to go elsewhere, we would still need the songbooks to fan away as much West-Texas summer heat as possible.

The annual revival was a time for most of Haskell to pull together. Friday-night football was the only thing that exceeded revivals in generating community unity. I was always glad I was a Christian when the annual outdoor revival rolled around. There was little doubt that I was on "the winning side."

The old parsonage finally exceeded its liveability. The new one was constructed closer to the church building, thus leaving insufficient room for the outdoor tabernacle. It was not a crisis, because by the time the new parsonage was needed, we were having the annual revival in the sanctuary, and not always in the summer time. A volleyball net was put up for the youth group where the outdoor tabernacle had once been. By that time, I was older, and volleyball interested me as much as revivals, especially if it was co-ed volleyball. But even then, I can remember standing in position, waiting for a serve, and feeling a wave of evangelistic nostalgia sweep over me. We lost something when the annual outdoor revivals moved inside. Air conditioning was nice, but it could never replace the "wind of the Spirit."

39

The Old Switcheroo

I began singing in church when I was real young. I couldn't have been more than two or three years old. I would stand up on the Holy Communion rail. Mrs. Bell would begin the hymn on the piano, and I would add to the worship experience with a rendition of such favorites as "Blessed Assurance" or "I Come to the Garden Alone." I'm sure I didn't do this as often as it seems like I did, but I have vivid memories of standing on that railing (not an insignificant feat in and of itself) and singing my heart out to what I surely imagined to be a spell-bound congregation.

I have Nellie Ash to thank for this. When mom and dad moved into their new house at 500 South Avenue H in Haskell, with a new baby boy, the lot next door was vacant. Dad had purchased it, but had no plans for it. Troy and Nellie Ash had lived most of their married life out in the country, but Troy had decided to move the "place" into Haskell. He made dad an offer on the lot, and the next thing I knew, their house was being hoisted off a large flatbed trailer and onto the land.

Nellie played the piano at one of the Baptist churches in town, at a local nursing home, and for a makeshift quartet. The quartet "toured" the area singing at churches and singing conventions in such places as Matson and Paint Creek. Closer to home, Nellie would invite me to come over, climb up on her piano bench, and sing as she played some of the old gospel songs. I learned a lot of them by heart. And it wasn't long before Nellie was convinced I needed to sing in public.

Since Nellie was a Baptist, she didn't play at the Methodist services. That was Mrs. Bell's job. I'm not sure how she got connected to me going public with my singing talent.

But she did, and it was not long before I was invited to sing in church. I enjoyed it for a while, but even good things can go sour. Adults are not the only ones who can "burn out." I remember telling mom and dad one afternoon that I really didn't want to sing at church that night. But they reminded me that I had agreed to do so. And after all, a man's only as good as his word.

I sat near the front as the service unfolded, waiting for my time to sing. For some reason, Mrs. Bell had not shown up to play. But the pastor wanted me to go ahead and sing anyway—acapella. When it came time for me to do so, I made my way to the front of the church and climbed up on the Communion rail like always. And then it hit me. Mrs. Bell was not there. I was in control. I didn't have to sing what I'd originally told everyone I was going to sing. I could sing whatever I wanted to.

True artists were known for their flashes of inspiration. If they could have theirs, I could have mine. So, instead of singing what everyone thought I was going to sing, I started off with another number—what I thought was a pretty good rendition of "The Dark Town Strutters' Ball." I belted out the lyrics: "I'll be down to get you in a taxi, honey. You'd better be ready 'bout half past eight. Oh, honey, don't be late; I want to be there when the band starts playin'...."

I don't remember much after I sang, "I'll be down to get you in a taxi, honey...." As soon as dad realized what was going on, he shot out of the pew, ran up the aisle, snagged me off the rail with one arm, and we disappeared into the parking lot. My "be-hind" glowed red, and I don't think we had to turn on the furnace that winter. We warmed ourselves by the heat coming from my butt. And...I am almost certain it was the last time I sang a solo in church.

40

Motley Crew

Before there was a rock group named "Motley Crue," there was the seventh grade football team at Haskell Junior High School. The senior high school team was named The Indians; the junior high school team was called The Warriors. Motley crew was a good description of what we looked like, and (truth be told) probably an indication of how we played.

My seventh-grade year was the first year Haskell ever had a junior high team. It actually began the year before when we were in the sixth grade. The coaches came over to elementary school and drilled us in the fundamentals of football. Apparently, we impressed them so much that they began to plan to keep us together when we migrated across town to junior high. Elementary-school recess was evolving into junior-high P.E.

In late July or early August, between our sixth and seventh-grade years, we received letters from the coaches telling us to report to the high school on a designated Saturday morning to get our football equipment. At the appointed hour, we lined up outside the old gymnasium while Coach Middleton literally crawled under the bleachers to retrieve equipment which had been stored there longer than anyone imagined.

From underneath the stands, he would call out the name of a piece of equipment (e.g. "left shoulder pad") and toss it out to whoever was at the front of the line. The idea was to pick up the pieces Coach Middleton threw out until you had a complete set—then, move out of the line so the next person could get his equipment. If Coach happened to throw out two pieces of the same item, the next person in line got a head start on his set.

I thought we did pretty good. Most of us got complete sets the first time around, but a few had to go around again until the necessary item was found and thrown out to the waiting team member. It was dark and hot underneath the grandstand, but Coach Middleton was relentless in his pursuit of items and we were patient in our willingness to wait until we had accumulated what we needed. To this day, I can remember the smell of the pieces he threw our way. They had been under there a long time, and by the looks of most items it was a wonder why they were ever saved in the first place. But it was all we had, and we were glad to have enough pieces to start the season.

My helmet was yellow with a black stripe running in the middle from front to back. No face mask. The chin strap didn't really go with the helmet, because Coach Middleton threw it out separately. But I was able to make it work. By the time I had picked up all the other pieces, I realized the seventh-grade, junior-high Warrior team was literally being created out of leftovers.

The only items in short supply were jerseys and pants. Only a few guys at the front of the line got them. The rest of us had to fend for ourselves. Coach Middleton's counsel was for us to go to Abilene and find them at Mackey's Sporting Goods store. That's all he told us, and that's what we did. Dad, mom, and I made a fast trip to Abilene, and I came back with a beautiful orange-and-black, long-sleeved jersey and khaki-colored pants. We also had to buy our shoes, and I selected high tops, like the ones Dandy Don wore.

We practiced in some old, white sweat shirts and pants that the coaches had scrounged from somewhere. That meant we didn't actually see each other in our "game uniforms" until the night of our opening bout with the Rule Bobcats. I have to tell the rest of this story through the eyes of my mom, because as actual team members, we were not overly concerned with appearances. We just wanted to win.

But this is precisely where the phrase motley crew came into the picture. When the Bobcats ran onto the field, they were wearing crisp, new uniforms with blue numbers on white jerseys. Their brand-new, white pants had blue stripes down the sides. Their helmets were glistening white. The Bobcats were "first class" from top to bottom.

We, on the other hand, came onto the field with a menagerie of colors and styles which apparently defied description. No two players looked the same. We could tell the Warriors from the Bobcats simply on the basis of appearance. We would hand the ball, or throw it, to the person wearing the hodge-podge uniform. We played our hearts out on that field. I don't remember who won. But as we were giving it all we had, our mothers were in the stands planning an "emergency chili supper" fund-raiser. Before the end of the season we had new uniforms.

41

Practice Snap

As I walked into seventh-grade science class, Coach Browning (who was also the junior-high science teacher) motioned for me to come up to his desk. When I got within earshot, he said, "Do you realize you could have been killed last night?" Oblivious to what he meant, I said, "No."

This was one of the most crucial exchanges I have ever had in my life, even though I didn't realize it at the time. In order for you to grasp the significance of the moment with Coach Browning, I have to take you back about fourteen hours earlier. I was the second-string quarterback for the Warriors. That in itself is important for you to know, because we really didn't have a second string. In other words, I was *bad*.

No one ever said it out loud, but I think my actual role on the team was to serve as a practice dummy for the rest of the players to block and tackle as we approached our next game. Our school district didn't have a big athletic budget, so the way I now see it, they needed people like me to suit up for afternoon practice sessions and let other people run over us. On game nights, I and the other practice dummies stood on the sidelines watching the same team members run over opposing players.

This is not to say I never played a real game. I was put in when we were so far ahead that we could not possibly lose....or....so hopelessly behind that we could not possibly win. The coaches usually didn't make that judgment until the last two minutes of the game, so I have very few memories of ever being on the field before then—except for the warm-up exercises prior to the kickoff.

Apart from ability, my biggest deficit was size. I was, and am, short. Truth be told, I was too small for football—certainly too small to be a quarterback—but most of my friends were on the team, and I could not imagine not being on it with them. Besides, Haskell did not have an abundant crop of possible players. So, in a strange way, I was needed. The problem was, I could never call a pass play. When the linemen stood up to block, I could not see over them to throw to the receiver. Whenever I went into the game, everyone knew the Warriors would only be executing running plays.

On the night before the infamous conversation with Coach Browning, I was in my usual place on the sideline. Suddenly, I heard Coach Middleton call out my name. "Harper!' he said, "get in there." I was so surprised that, to this day, I don't remember if we were winning or losing. All I remember was how cold it was that night....real cold.... extremely COLD.

As the game had progressed to within two minutes of its end, my hands and fingers were numb, blocks of stone at the end of my arms. Not a good thing for a quarterback.

Running onto the field, I could not remember the last time I had taken a snap from the center. It had been days. The feel of the old pigskin popping into my hands was just a distant memory. But I knew what to do. I was confident. Everything would be okay. After I called my play and triumphantly marched the team up to the line of scrimmage, I called out, "Practice snap!"

In that moment, time stood still—all over the world, I think. The opposing linemen, who were already down in their lunge positions, looked puzzled. Some of my own teammates moved their heads enough to give me odd facial expressions. But I had taken control of the moment. Frankie Don White followed my orders and snapped me the ball. Ah, the football!

I felt its ridges and seams. I rolled it around in my hands. I pumped my half-frozen arm a time or two to loosen it up. I gave the ball back to Frankie Don, and we ran the play. For some reason, Coach Middleton immediately screamed from the sideline, "Harper, get back here!" That was my only play of the night.

Coach Browning had been refereeing the game. That's the way teams did it for junior high games in those days. Each team appointed a coach to be a referee. That seemed fair enough, and it worked for us. Coach Browning had called the game, and he had been doing his job when I made my brief appearance on the field. When I came in for class the next morning, he told me, "I didn't know what to do. I didn't know whether to blow the whistle, throw the penalty flag, or what."

It was only then that I realized there is no such thing in football as a "practice snap." The ball was in play the moment

Frankie Don snapped it to me. But the night before, and for only one time in the school's history, at Indian Stadium in Haskell, there was such a thing. There was a practice snap. I know this for sure; I was there when it happened.

42

Bounced Back

It only took me one year to figure out my football career was terminal. It was one thing to be "Dandy Don" on Saturdays in Bill Perry's front yard; it was something entirely different to be the second-string quarterback for the Warriors. As my eighth-grade year began, I offered my services to Coach Middleton to be the team manager. With amazing speed, he took me up on my offer.

It was a good deal. I got to attend all the games. I traveled on the bus with the rest of the team. And at the end-of-the-year awards' ceremony, I received a letter jacket just like everyone else. Long gone were the days of being blocked and tackled all week during practice sessions, but seeing virtually no action during the games. Now, I was "in charge" of making sure the players were taped up and ready to go, and I was the person who took water to them on the field during the timeouts.

Since there's no one else here to do it, I have to tell you that I was pretty good at my job, even though I would never claim perfection. I can still remember the night when Coach Middleton acted as if he wanted to throw me across the field when I put an ammonia capsule under the nose of a downed player. I learned (quickly) that you DO NOT do that to someone who might have a neck or back injury—even if they're woozy. I learned other things through "on the job training." But Coach Middleton never fired me. In fact, I remained the team manager through my senior year in high school.

Even managers have their "moment of glory." And I had mine. Another cold night. I was in high school and had moved up to working as the B-Team Manager. We were the Indians now. Next year, most of the team would become the A-

Team, and I would go with them. For now, we gave it our all on Thursday nights, not the A-Team's Friday-night schedule. But it would be a B-Team game night when my "moment of glory" occurred.

Our team had called a time out. It was my job to have a case of Coke bottles filled with water and ready to be carried out to the team. These were pre Gatorade days, the days before the plastic bottles with the long spouts. Just twenty four Coke bottles in a yellow, wooden case, filled and ready to go.

Coach Middleton had trained the team to take their time outs in a corporate kneeling position—a large circle in which each player rested his hands on his right knee and placed his helmet next to his left knee. It was impressive. My job—should I choose to accept it—was to deliver the bottles to each player as quickly as possible. No sweat. I had done it many times before.

Just grab the hand holes on each end of the yellow case and head out onto the field. Nothing to it.

Well...one problem. Until that moment, I had never noticed that you cannot see your feet when you are running with a Coke case in your hands. But even if you could, your gaze would not be on your feet; it would be on the field and the players you were speeding forth to serve. Furthermore, I had not recalled that a chain is connected to each of the yard markers—a chain that is largely hidden in the grass, and pulled tight to establish the ten-yard journey the team has to make in no more than four plays.

As I raced from the sideline onto the field, I ran between the yard markers and tripped over the chain. I was going full throttle when I hit the ground with my Coke case. The sound of me slamming onto the field with twenty four glass bottles brought an instant "oh, no!" sound from the crowd on the home-team side of the field. I remember that sound to this day.

But—and I swear this is true—as quickly as I had fallen, I was up on my feet, completing my mission. I bounced in a way that enabled me not even to break stride. I had not lost a bottle or spilled a drop. The entire Coke case was intact. I went on to perform my routine with skill and professionalism, being sure that each team member quenched his thirst and regained his energy. And as I retrieved the empty bottles, placed them back into the yellow case, and headed toward the sideline, the entire home-team crowd rose to their feet and gave me a standing ovation. It was my finest hour!

43

Two Points

Just as Winter follows Fall, basketball followed football in Haskell. It was a seasonal reality, but also a practical necessity. We didn't have enough athletes to play two different sports simultaneously, or enough money to pay coaches who specialized in only one sport. So, just as the junior-high Warriors had a football team, we also had a junior-high basketball team which used the same name.

Keep in mind that if I was too short to play football, it goes without saying that I was too short for basketball. But as with football, all my friends were playing, so I suited up as well. I was not good, but when lumped in with the whole team, I came in at about seventh or eighth in quality. This meant that I spent most of my time on the bench, as I had in football. Coach

Middleton tried to see that every player got some game time. Mine typically came when one of our "big shooters" (defined in the context of seventh and eighth-grade basketball) needed a rest. It could happen anytime during the game, but it didn't last very long.

I scored three points. I don't mean that I "averaged" three points per game; I mean I *scored* three points---three points over a two-season period. In the seventh grade I made a foul shot, and in the eighth-grade, I made a field goal. Three points. It's the field goal that I want to tell you about.

Apparently, I had been showing some promise in my eighth-grade year, because Coach Middleton was putting me into the game more often. In fact, I played so much that I had to wash my uniform after the game. I became Coach Middleton's first sub, even though my scoring remained as I have described it in the paragraph above. I was fast and I could "get in the face" (more accurately, in the chest) of opposing players. I can only imagine what I looked like with my arms flailing in desperate attempts to keep them from scoring.

And that's where the point of this story begins. I have not gone to a lot of trouble to check out the facts. Some things are best kept the way *you* remember them. All I can tell you is that in one game in my eighth-grade season, I scored a field goal. Two points. Two points that changed my basketball career. I shot the ball with all the finesse I had, and "swoosh," it went through the hoop—nothing but net. We went on to win the game. I like to think we won by two points.

As we walked toward the locker room, Coach Middleton came up to me and said, "Harper, you played a really good game tonight. I've decided to start you tomorrow morning at the tournament in Paint Creek." He gave me a coach-like pat on the butt and walked away, leaving me to ponder what he had said.

For a moment, I thought I had misunderstood—you know, crowd noise and everything else going on. But I asked my friend, Perry Turnbow, and he verified that Coach Middleton had used the word "start" and my name in the same sentence.

Start? Start! I had never heard Coach Middleton say those words in reference to me! Start? Start! It began to soak in. I would take to the court in the opening seconds of the tournament game in the morning. I would be a "starter." My excitement swelled, and during the night, so did my face. I woke up the next morning with the mumps!

44

Golf Is My Game

"If at first you don't succeed…." These words must have been spoken by someone who tried junior-high football and basketball—and failed. My talents had congealed in Little League and Pony League baseball, played in the summertime. I have to tell you that I was a pretty good baseball player. Being short was not an automatic deficiency. In fact, it had some advantages. But when it came to playing sports during the regular school year, the only option I had besides football, basketball, and track was golf.

The Haskell County Country Club was built when I was around ten years old. My dad was on the charter Board of Directors, so we made regular trips out north of town to check on construction progress. Ed Hester had sold some of his property to the county for the golf course. It was a big deal for Haskell. When we would drive out for a look, dad would say things like, "Here is where the first green will be."

In the early trips, I had to take dad's word for it, and use my imagination to connect stakes, string, and little ribbons blowing in the wind with the eventual outcome. But as the weeks went by, what he originally predicted in words began to take shape in the dirt of what had previously been one of Ed Hester's cow pastures.

In time, there it was! The most beautiful nine-hole golf course I had ever seen—in fact, the only one I'd ever seen. Soon after it opened, and thanks to the Montgomery Ward catalog, dad and I had our own sets of golf clubs. Dad's was a full set; mine included only two woods (a "one" and a "three"), four irons (3, 5, 7, and 9), a putter, and a red bag. I added three Pinnacle golf balls. I was on my way to stardom!

Somewhere around my sophomore year in high school, Coach Middleton decided the time was right for the Indians to add a golf team to their sporting events. Other area schools were doing likewise, and we would compete with many of the same towns and athletes that we had in the other sports. When Coach put the word out that he needed to recruit a team, I was there with my red bag ready to offer my services. And I made the team—fair and square. I was the fifth person Coach Middleton selected to make up a team comprised of five players. I have a picture in my high-school annual to prove what I am telling you.

We played tournaments each Spring. The big one was in Stamford, our chief rival school in all sports, and a town that had had a golf course for quite a while. Schools in our district converged on the Stamford links for the championship event. For the first time in my life, I was introduced over a loud speaker as I teed up for my opening drive. "Now teeing off for the Haskell Indians....Steve Harper!"

The next 30 seconds live in eternity. I retrieved the one-wood out of my bag and took the customary two or three warm-up swings. Slow and easy. With confidence. Almost casual. I pushed my tee into the soft dirt on the tee box, addressed the ball, put my head down, and adjusted my stance with the necessary preliminary hip action. One final flex of the fingers on the club handle. Then, a firm grip.

I executed what felt like a textbook swing. But I must have raised up just a tad, because I nearly whiffed the ball. I dribbled it off the front of the tee box—to be generous, I'll say five yards. This shot was the last of four drives launched in my group. Most were over two hundred yards down the fairway, hardly visible from the tee box. My shot was still in plain sight, with the ball looking about the same size it did when I teed it up a few moments ago.

For those of you unfamiliar with the game of golf, let me inform you that I was now "hitting two" (my second shot) almost as far away from the green as when I began. I was still in full view of everyone gathered around the first tee to watch players begin their day. I was close enough to hear them gasp and comment about my drive. I should have taken that as an omen for the rest of the day, but I played on...undaunted.

The Stamford course had something on it that no other course in the district had—water hazards. We had a couple of ravines on the Haskell course, and when it rained a lot, they had water in them. But nothing that had water all the time. When they had some water in them, or were muddy, we allowed golfers to drop out with no penalty and play on. The Stamford course had three bonafide "water holes."

I could write about this in more detail, but it's too painful. The gist is that by the time I arrived at the third water hole, I only had two golf balls left. Honestly, I do not know how many I started the round with, but it was roughly a "bag full." Again, for those of you who do not know much about golf, I have to tell you that each time you lose a ball (in the water or the rough), you have to take a penalty stroke, which means that your score moves ever higher as you go from hole to hole. Losing a "bag full" of balls is not a good thing.

It really doesn't matter how many golf balls I started with, for soon, I had none. My final two balls sailed into the water. I had to beg one of the other players to give me one of his balls—which he only agreed to do if I hit it from the other side of the water hazard. I had no choice but to comply, and I limped into the clubhouse a couple of holes later with a score of 65 on the first nine holes.

At an official high-school tournament, each player must sign his card in the presence of a score keeper. The score is then posted on a large scoreboard for everyone else to see. When I walked up to the scorer's table, no one was there. So, I simply signed my card, left it in plain sight for the score keeper when he returned, and went into the clubhouse for a Coke.

When I came outside, the score keeper was back, and he was standing up to write my score of "65" on the big board. It stood alongside 37's, 41's, etc. As I passed by the scoring table, he turned to me and asked, "Who in the world is this Harper guy from Haskell?" I looked him straight in the eye and replied in a firm voice, "Beats me. I've never heard of him before in my life!"

45

Electric Baseball

Baseball was "big stuff" in Haskell in the fifties. Little League started about the time I was old enough to play, and it grew up along with us, moving forward to include Pony League. Every summer for twelve years, I played along with more kids than played any other sport during the year. We had a kind of minor league for the youngest players. I began my baseball career on the Cats. But in a couple of years, everyone went on to Little League proper, being assigned to the Rams, Hawks, Bears, or Tigers. I was sent to the Rams, playing there until high school when some of us moved up to Pony League. We only had one "Haskell" team at that level.

You could not play baseball year-round, because the sport wasn't offered in the school system, and the winters were too cold. But Bill Perry and I had a way to keep the game going throughout the year. We each bought an electric baseball game and invented our own season. For several years, our Saturdays included playing a game at either my house, or Bill's.

Actually, it didn't really begin with electric baseball, but with baseball cards. Bill and I got ours at Trice's Grocery, just a few blocks from his house. Trice's Grocery would today be in the category of a convenience store, but we didn't have that term in those days. It was just a small store on the north side of town, and among the items that Mr. Trice sold were baseball cards. About once a week, each of us gathered the necessary $1.05 and purchased a complete box of cards.

A box of baseball cards contained one hundred cards, individually wrapped, with a piece of thin, flat, and pink bubblegum included with the card of a particular major-league player. The first thing we did was to throw away most of the gum, which even to us in those days was brittle and not as tasty as the stand-alone bubble gum you could buy for a penny a piece. Besides, it was difficult to chew your way through one hundred pieces of gum in a week. We could never have done that without sending our jaws into a permanent spasm, to say nothing of its effect on our teeth.

So, we'd get our box of cards from Mr. Trice and head for the garbage can just outside the front door. We'd dump most of the gum, but pop a couple of pieces into our mouths to chew on while we were opening and examining the cards we'd bought that week. By the time we'd purchased several years' worth of weekly boxes, our collection was virtually complete. Our search was for new players, for special-issue cards, for an elusive player we didn't have, or for the annual team card with related stats. Bill specialized in the Dodgers (Brooklyn and later

Los Angeles), and I zeroed in on the Yankees. Our goal was to collect complete teams each year.

I must insert a brief interlude into this story—one that has only become apparent to me in my adult years. One of my memories (nightmares?) is of Bill and me standing beside Mr. Trice's garbage can, not only throwing excess bubble gum into it, but also duplicate cards. For those of you who are serious baseball-card collectors, I hope this doesn't cause you to pass out. But I have memories of throwing away duplicates of such players as Stan Musial, Willie Mays, Ted Williams, etc. In the trash they'd go, if we already had that card. Can you believe it!

Now back to the story—if you're still conscious. With our teams in hand, and with plenty of gum to chew week after week, we returned home to play electric baseball. We pulled out the nine players for that day's game, arranged them in their batting order, and (in our own way) declared "play ball." For the next couple of hours we were pitching, hitting, fielding, and running. We played a complete season (as we defined it) and even had a World Series at the end of it. Mind you, it was always games between the Yankees and the Dodgers, but a World Series was called for anyway.

Just in case you haven't ever seen an electric-baseball game, let me describe it. The game board itself was metal, about two-feet square, maybe slightly larger. It included the infield, the outfield, a little bit of foul territory behind the plate and down each base line. There was also a metal piece sticking up in the outfield, to simulate the fence and a make-believe grandstand.

Attached to the field were nine metal players, slotted into their respective positions. The pitcher's mound was the heart of the game, and it was actually where the "electric" part came in. Sticking out of the metal playing field at the mound was a sort of "arm" that could throw a tiny white magnetic ball toward the batter. It "threw" whenever the operator, whose team was on the field, pushed a button that ignited the electricity and created a magnetic field, which launched the little white ball toward the plate.

The game came with a bat attached to the left of home plate, where (hopefully) the other player could hit what had just been thrown. The bat had a spring device, so that when you pulled it back (in anticipation of the pitch) and then let it go as the ball came toward you, the bat would "swing" and hit the ball. If you did hit the pitch, you hoped that you timed it in a way that the little white magnetic ball did not fly into, or roll onto one of the silver, metal players on the field...or fall within a circle drawn around each player. If the ball landed in a safe place, it was a hit. If it stuck to one of the players or fell inside the respective circle, you were out. If you hit a long, fly-ball that stuck to the bleachers in the outfield, it was a home run. You get the picture.

But, back to the bat. If the pitcher's mound was the power center, the bat was (to our way of thinking) the problem. Most obviously, it was on the left-side of home plate, which meant that it technically only served right-handed hitters. Not every baseball-card athlete hit right-handed. It just didn't seem right to ask a "lefty" to bat right-handed. Furthermore, Bill and I knew (since we played Little League baseball) that bats are not fastened to the ground or connected to springs. No sir, you hold a bat and you have to swing it yourself if you hope to get a hit. So, we agreed to remove the bat from its spring-loaded base on each of our games and hold it in our fingers as the opposing pitcher pushed the button and sent the little white magnetic ball hurling toward the batter.

In this way we could pull up the next baseball-card batter and he could swing either right-handed, left-handed, or even as a switch-hitter. We had immediately "improved" electric baseball. But there was another problem lurking that could have destroyed the whole thing. With the bat no longer attached to the game board or being spring-loaded, it was possible to hold the little bat and swing it in a manner that almost always resulted in a home run.

We called it "scooping." It was a well-timed, sharp, upward motion of the little bat that created a fly ball with enough speed to virtually guarantee that it would either stick to the metal bleachers in the outfield—or maybe go out of the stadium altogether. But since home runs don't happen that often in real baseball, we had to make a rule that there would be no "scooping" by the batter. You had to keep the bat on the game board and swing it with a twist of your fingers. No scooping.

Looking back on our years of electric baseball, I remember those games as being some of the most fun Bill and I ever had. Our generation seems to have been particularly blessed. Dad's generation didn't have electric baseball, and my son and his friends never played it. But there was a "moment in time" when you could ride your bike to Trice's Grocery, purchase one hundred cards for $1.05, throw away the duplicates, save enough gum to enjoy, and then head back home for a great game. When I thank God for His goodness, I include being a kid when electric baseball was around.

46

Which Way Did He Go?

When a boy turned seven, a special rite-of-passage occurred. He was eligible to play Little League baseball. This was what many of us used to survive summers in Haskell. We went to the local Western Auto store to pick out a baseball glove and then around the square to Wheatley's Ready To Wear for baseball shoes. The next step was to learn which team we'd been assigned to. A few weeks before school was out for the summer, teams would begin to practice. The actual season was in June and July.

I turned seven in October, so it felt like "forever" before I learned that I had been assigned to the Cats. I already had my glove and shoes. In fact, dad and I had been going across the street to the elementary-school playground, where he would hit grounders and fly balls to me until either he or I was worn out. Also, the "Avenue H Gang" had been playing baseball in Bill Perry's backyard for a year or two.

Years later, I drove to Bill Perry's house, now owned by someone else, to see that original back-yard baseball field. I was astonished at how small it is, compared to how big it seemed at the time. But it might as well have been Yankee Stadium. It served us well, complete with an outfield fence that eliminated all debate as to whether a batter had hit a home run, or not. All this to say—by the time the summer of my seventh year rolled around, I was ready to play Little League.

Each team was sponsored by a local business. The Cats were sponsored by Brazelton Lumber Company. That fact was printed in yellow on the back of each purple, short-sleeved jersey. On the front, "The Cats" was printed on the upper left side and the player's number (number "7" for me) on the lower right side. We also had a purple cap with a yellow "C" glued onto it. Pants were left to the discretion of each player, which meant Blue Jeans for most of us. No matching baseball socks at that stage of things.

Some of us had played on neighborhood teams like the one in Bill Perry's back yard. Perry Turnbow and Wylie White were already good for their age, along with some others. Perry could "smoke" a batter with his fastball, and Wylie played a mean second base. I took my place in center field. Ronnie Joselett played left field, and Randy Wiseman flanked me in right.

It's Randy that I want to tell you about. He was one of those guys who had not prepared for Little League by being on a neighborhood team. So, right field was his position. Ninth was his batting order. But it didn't really matter, Randy was our friend. He was a Cat as much as anyone else was, and truth be told, probably not that much worse than the rest of us!

When the practice phase was over, we moved into our first season, and Randy came to his first time at bat. Even though he had been at the plate before the season began, it was different batting in an actual game. We all felt the pressure, and Randy was not the only nervous player on the team that day. He watched the first two "stee-rikes" go by, with some additional "balls", no doubt. From the dugout, we were all screaming, "Swing, Randy, swing!"

Apparently he heard us, for that's exactly what he did when the next pitch came his way. And...he hit the ball, a grounder trickling out toward second base, just a little faster than a bunt. He was so surprised to realize that he'd made contact with it, he just stood there watching the ball roll on the ground—the way someone might stand still to gaze at a great work of art in a museum.

From the dugout, we were yelling, "Run, Randy, run!" Since he'd followed our exhortation to swing, maybe he'd do the same thing with respect to running. And as before, he heard us. Our shouting awakened him from the daze, and Randy ran...my, how he ran...as fast as he could, with his head down, his arms waving and his feet flying...toward third base!

47

Right Field

Peter, Paul, and Mary were one of our favorite groups growing up in Haskell. Their well-known song, "Right Field," could have been inspired by things that happened to Little Leaguers I played with in the fifties. Randy Wiseman was not always my companion out in right field. In fact, when we moved up to the next level, he was assigned to the Bears, not the Rams. When the older, more-experienced Rams took to the field, Marvin Gregory was our usual right fielder.

Marvin was, and still is, my friend. His dad managed the local Piggly Wiggly grocery store, so our family and the Gregory's go way back. When Marvin was born, it was not long before his parents, and a lot of other people in Haskell as well, knew that he was a genius—really. He still is. I vividly recall the picture in The Haskell Free Press, with little Marvin sitting on the floor reading a book long before kids were supposed to be able to read.

I remember the day we picked him up to go to one of our practice sessions. Mom honked the horn outside his front door, and Marvin emerged in a minute or so. When he settled into the back seat, I asked him what he had been doing that afternoon. Marvin replied, "Drawing a schematic of the water system of Haskell." (Silence) There didn't seem to be any need to tell him what I had been doing. Marvin was smart, real smart. Marvin played right field.

The Rams were playing a night game. I was in center field, Marvin in right. All of a sudden, my dad came running out of the dugout, waving his arms, and hollering to the umpire, "Time out! Time out!" This got our attention immediately, because he had never done that before—and I don't think he ever did it again. Every eye in the stadium followed him as he raced toward—right field—toward Marvin. Time seemed to stand still…and then, I saw it. Marvin had his cap pulled over his face, with his glove perched on top of his head. His neck was craned backward, and he was looking out of the little holes in his cap, into the sky.

When dad got to Marvin, he said in a tone of voice that fit his bewilderment, "Marvin! *What… are… you… doing?*" Marvin slowly peeked out from under his cap, and with the same calm, matter-of-fact response he had used in answering my question in the car, he told my dad, "I am seeing how many different varieties of bugs I can identify in the lights."

Right field. Peter, Paul, and Mary wrote a song about it. But I stood next to Marvin in it. A good place to watch the dandelions grow, they said. A gcod place to identify bug species, Marvin said. For me, a good place to make a memory

and a friend.

48

The Mick

I've already told you that I played center field in Little League and Pony League, from first grade all the way through my senior year in high school. This was no accident. It has to do with my parentage and my birthday. My dad was a die-hard New York Yankee's fan all his life. And I was born on the same day as Mickey Mantle, October 20th. I collected every baseball card of him I could find over the years, as well as magazines and other memorabilia.

To this day, not far from where I am writing this, I have a plastic Mickey Mantle figurine, with him posed in a left-handed batting position. To make the doll more correct, the first day I had it, I took a Papermate ballpoint pen with blue ink and filled in the pinstripes on his uniform. The "Antique Road

Show" value has been compromised, but no true Yankee would stand for a uniform without blue pinstripes.

Along with him, I could name the rest of the team. Yogi Berra, catcher. Bill Skowron at first. Bobby Richardson at second. Toney Kubek at shortstop. Gil Hodges at third. Elston Howard in left field, and Roger Maris in right. Several pitchers might be on the mound—Whitey Ford being my personal favorite. Annual trips to Trice's Grocery kept these heroes up-to-date in my baseball card collection.

But way above them all was "the Mick." Before I ever wore "Number 7" on my Cats' Little League jersey, I had written it in Crayola on a white tee shirt as a member of Bill Perry's back-yard team. Dad found me a Yankee cap, which I completely wore out. I had a Louisville Slugger bat with his autograph on it. I don't think I missed a game on television that he played in.

So, there was no doubt what position I'd play. Unlike my deficiencies when applied to football, basketball, and golf, I was a pretty good baseball player...and, if I do say so myself...an especially good center fielder. I was quick. Dad had hit me a million fly balls on the elementary school playground, so that I could catch them the way Mickey did— camping under a "tall can of corn" or snagging a line drive on the run. If I had been a better batter, I might have entertained the idea of playing baseball for a career. Or at least it seemed so at the time.

Mantle was my inspiration. Who will ever forget his unbelievable catch in the World Series' that saved Don Larsen's perfect game? And he did it with great pain, running on legs that he had to tape up just to use them. I can still see him limping to and from the outfield...game after game...year after year. And when he came to bat, he had a stance I did my best to copy. I even tried my hand at switch-hitting, but it was not to be.

I never saw him play a game in person. By the time Dallas got the Texas Rangers as an American-League franchise team, Mickey had retired. As close as I ever got to him in those days was when dad and I made a special trip to roll a few games at the Mickey Mantle Bowling Lanes that he owned in east Dallas. Mickey wasn't there, but there were pictures of him I'd never seen before. We even stayed in a motel named after him next to the bowling alley. I always hoped to meet him.

Years passed. I grew up, left Haskell, got married, graduated from college and seminary, had children, pastored a while in Texas, completed my Ph.D. at Duke, and moved to Kentucky to be a professor at Asbury Theological Seminary. Now and then, I'd read or hear something about Mickey, but I lost track of him for the most part.

Then, one day, the Lexington Herald-Leader newspaper advertised a Book Fair to be held soon in Frankfort, only about a half-hour from Wilmore. Mickey Mantle was to be the featured guest and book signer. Instantly, the inner voice said, "You *will* go there and meet Mickey Mantle." It was predestined. I packed up Jeannie, John, and Katrina in the car, and we headed out to the fair. Sure enough, there he was at the signing table, autographing copies of his new autobiography, *The Mick.* The line moved quickly, and I knew I'd only have a moment to be near him.

When I put my copy of the book down on the table for him to sign, he wrote on the cover page: "To Steve. Best Wishes. Mickey Mantle." Jeannie snapped a photo as he did so, capturing an angle that made it appear we were close friends. All those years in center field in Haskell were worth that moment.

49

The Last Out

Endings are never easy. This was especially true of my final game of baseball. For twelve seasons I had donned a uniform—for the Cats, Rams, or the Indians. It was nearly impossible to think of summer without baseball, even though I was moving on to college. McMurry didn't have a baseball team at the time; otherwise, I would probably have tried out.

Over the years, our core team had jelled. We had been playing together for a dozen years, either with or against each other. The final Pony League team, the Indians, was made up of those of us who had decided to play baseball as long as we could. So, we really did have a "team spirit." We had learned a lot about baseball, but more importantly, we had learned a lot about ourselves. We had a sense that something very special was coming to an end as we took the field for our final game.

It was the bottom of the seventh—the last inning in a Pony League game. We were trailing 3 to 2. When I came to bat, I hit a single. Bill Perry followed me in the cleanup slot. I represented the tying run on first, and Bill was the winning run at the plate. Bill's reputation as a clutch hitter was well-known; we were feeling confident that the game was far from over. All those years in Bill's backyard, and all the years since in Little League and Pony League came to focus in that moment.

Two outs. Avoid the force out at second at all costs. All we needed was a single far enough into the outfield to give me time to head for home plate. I could make it. I was fast. And sure enough—crack! Bill rifled a line drive into left field that hit the fence on the fly, a cinch double, maybe a triple. I had enough time to even crawl home on my hands and knees. Extra innings, at least, here we come! Things were looking good for the Indians.

But rounding second base, I missed the bag. I knew if anyone saw me, all they had to do was call for the ball and tag the base. I'd be out, and the game would be over. We would lose a heart breaker. All that was whirling through my mind when I failed to feel my foot touch the base, and I continued on toward third.

Somewhere roughly halfway between second and third, I threw on the brakes and headed back to touch second. I'd convinced myself that I couldn't risk being found out. Twelve years of playing baseball had taught me better, but the thought of someone simply calling for the ball and tagging the base was more than I could accept in that critical moment. So, I turned on my heels and headed back to second base.

About the time I made it back there, Bill was arriving. I'm sure he figured I was in the dugout cooling it, but no—I was right there in front of him. The look on his face was indescribable, and all he could get out of his voice was a weak and bewildered, "What are you doing here, Harp?" Good question. I really didn't know.

By this time, the left fielder had retrieved the ball and thrown it to the third baseman, who was now sort of playing catch with himself, waiting for me to get there. His position between me and the base was his way of daring me to make it. I did my best, but it was futile. Like a bull who has been pierced in the heart by the matador's sword, I was dead on my feet. He tagged me out. The game was over. We lost 3 to 2. I discovered that no one had seen me miss second base. I would have been home free.

Some years later, I saw Bill Perry when I went back to Haskell for a visit. I asked him if he remembered that night. He did, and he still does. To this day, when we talk about that last out, he says the same thing, "You know, Harp, you're just too honest!"

50

When TV Came to Town: Reprise

I've already told you that when our family purchased a television, we made Park Woodsen a happy man. We bought a Zenith. He had to order the particular model that dad selected. More than once, Park told us it should be in "any day now."

It arrived on a Saturday when Perry Turnbow was having his birthday party in the city park. Park had called to say the TV would be delivered sometime that day. I made mom promise she would come get me if it arrived at the house while I was at Perry's party. Sure enough, she pulled up near a side gate where we were playing, eating cake, and opening presents. She waved to me to get into the car; they were unloading the TV at the house.

This was not a calloused departure. Everyone already knew the TV was being delivered that day, and they understood my need to leave. The Pope would have understood if it had happened while I was having an audience with him. Besides, I promised to give a full report at school on Monday.

When I walked into the house, the television was already sitting in the place we'd reserved for it in the living room. The delivery men were now on our roof installing the antenna and hooking it up to the console. Several days earlier, they had set the antenna pole in a cement-filled hole in the ground just outside our back door. I ran into the backyard to watch the technicians attach the antenna to the pole and turn it toward the direction where it would pick up the station in Abilene.

Everything was set. Park Woodsen showed up to personally go over the owner's manual with us. He went page-by-page, showing us what the knobs were for and how to use them. Then he left. We were now ready for some "real television" in our home! No more trips downtown to watch TV's in store windows or finding excuses to go to the Couch's to watch their TV. We had our own television!

KRBC was on the air, broadcasting its ever-popular "cooking show" live and direct from the station. When the Cub Scout Den went to the Calvin Kiwi Show, I saw the kitchen in one corner of the studio. Who would have imagined that human beings would sit transfixed in front of a television screen while a stranger told viewers how to prepare Swiss steak? But that's what we did. That's what everybody did in Haskell—when TV came to town.